A Novel by Nicholas Edwards
Based on the Motion Picture from Hollywood Pictures
Co-Executive Producer Michael Rotenberg
Executive Producer Hilton Green
Based on the screenplay by Shawn Schepps
From a story by George Zaloom & Shawn Schepps
Produced by George Zaloom
Directed by Les Mayfield

SCHOLASTIC INC.
New York Toronto London Auckland Sydney

ISBN 0-590-45978-3

12 11 10 9 8 7 6 5 4 3 2 1   2 3 4 5 6 7/9

Printed in the U.S.A.   01

First Scholastic printing, June 1992

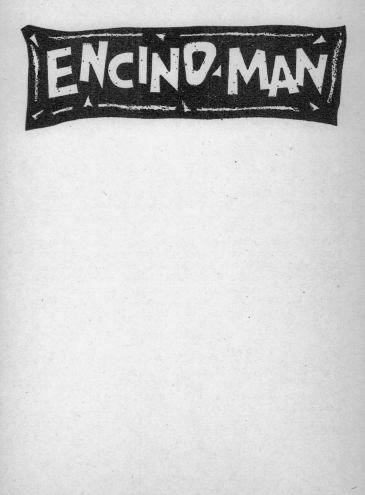

Chapter 1

It was a world that once was, in a time we will never know, and can only imagine. The eerie sounds of long-extinct wild animals echoed across the icy tundra, and into a deep valley surrounded by glaciers.

It was dusk, and the land was deserted.

Except for . . . a caveman, and a cavewoman, shivering in the cold outside their cave. They were bundled up in full animal fur suits, but the cavewoman's teeth chattered as the temperature dropped along with the sun. Her hairdo was wild — but, oddly, looked just like the big-hair of any modern surf-rock chick.

Seeing how cold she was, the caveman gathered up two sticks and began to rub them together, trying to start a fire to ward off the evening chill. He rubbed, and he rubbed, and he rubbed — and nothing happened. He growled, and dropped the sticks in frustration.

The cavewoman, hard at work grinding grain in a prehistoric bowl, looked over and laughed.

The caveman sighed, picked up the sticks, and tried again. Finally, the sticks began to smoke from the friction, and he rubbed harder, shielding the first little tongue of flame from the wind, and lighting a small pile of wood. He blew on the tinder and kindling until the flame caught, then sat back to watch the fire, pleased with himself.

The cave, inside and out, was covered with cave drawings of various animals, symbols, and scenes of the cavepeople's daily lives. Around the caveman's work area, there were crudely fashioned tools, and handmade hunting implements. Countless rocks had been formed into the shapes of octagons, pentagons, triangles, and an oblong round rock — the first stages in the development of the wheel.

As the caveman studied his oblong rock, trying to decide where — and why — to chip it next, the cavewoman walked over and kissed her caveman. When he didn't seem to notice, she threw some grain at him from her bowl. He looked up to see her smiling mischievously at him, and they both laughed. He pulled her down next to him, and they cooed and kissed.

It was prehistoric domestic bliss.

Suddenly, there was a low, rumbling echo from the cliff above them. Neither of them noticed as some ice cracked off from the top and fell to the rocks below.

The ground began to shake all around them. It was a terrible, roaring earthquake — the kind that legends are made of. The cavewoman was tossed by the mighty force away from the caveman, and he grabbed his spear and raised it threateningly towards the sky and the unknown gods who were causing this nightmare. He did a little dance with the spear, trying to ward off the evil spirits before he and his cavewoman came to any harm.

Just then, a tremendous avalanche of ice and snow buried them both.

The caveman's world no longer existed.

Chapter 2

In a present-day California bedroom, there was also an earthquake in progress. The walls and floor shook as books were knocked off a shelf filled with adolescent junk. There was a dusty ant farm, a half-filled soda can, a color snapshot of a boy and a girl about six years old playing and splashing around in a bathtub together, a Dodgers cap, and an expensive, if battered, camera. All of these possessions fell to the floor, creating their own avalanche.

Dave Morgan lay asleep in bed as the room around him shuddered, and more books tumbled from the shelf. A hamster in a cage on the desk fell off its wheel, landed in a pile of cedar shavings that covered the bottom of the cage, and blinked in obvious rodent surprise. Dave just tossed and turned in bed, still half asleep.

"Mom, quit it!" he mumbled, his face in his pillow. "I'm getting up."

There was a rather ugly jolt, and he sat up.

"Mom!" he said, exasperated.

He looked around his room in some confusion. Dave was seventeen and very energetic — once he was awake. He was the kind of guy who was hip in a way that was only going to be appreciated when he was about . . . thirty. So, at this stage of his life, Popularity wasn't exactly his middle name.

There was another nasty tremor, and he groaned, ducking a few more falling books, and pulled his covers up over his head.

"Dave?" his mother called from somewhere down the hall. "Are you okay?"

Dave just stayed under the covers, waiting for the tremor to subside.

"I hate those things," he said quietly, once the minor earthquake was over.

It was a typical — but not very pleasant — California way to wake up.

Dave's house looked very much like a place where the Beaver might have grown up. There was an old swing set rusting away in one corner of the yard, and a toolshed off to the side of the house. Everything about the property was status quo — with the exception of the large and deep hole in the middle of the yard.

Dirt came flying out of the hole at regular intervals, and a beat box sitting next to the growing pile of dirt blasted out cool — and loud — tunes as Dave dug in fast rhythm to the songs.

Stanley Brown — better known as Stoney — came running out of Dave's back door with a bagel in his mouth. He and Dave had been best friends since elementary school, and Stoney was more than a little eccentric. He was a true free spirit, who wore wild clothes, and saw life at a very different angle from the rest of the world.

"Stanley!" Dave's mother, Mrs. Morgan, yelled from the house. "Put that back!"

Stoney laughed, and skidded to a stop at the edge of the hole. He looked inside, chomping on the bagel as a fresh pile of dirt flew out and hit him in the face.

"Hey, bud-dy!" he protested, and wiped the dirt from his face and bagel.

Dave looked up, shovel in hand. "Sorry. What's my mom yelling about?"

Stoney grinned. "She's edged 'cause I snitched her last bagel."

Dave nodded, and went back to digging. "Grab a shovel," he said.

Stoney stepped dramatically away from the edge of the hole. "Not *even*. I wanta munch."

"Fine." Dave kept digging. "If you don't want to help, fine." He bent down with the shovel, tossing more dirt in Stoney's direction.

Stoney just ducked, and kept chewing his bagel.

The sliding glass doors to the backyard opened, and Teena, Dave's fifteen-year-old sister, came out of the house with two glasses of juice and a plate of Pop-Tarts. Boris, the family dog, followed her, nipping at her heels.

She put the juice and Pop-Tarts down by the side of the hole, avoiding another shower of dirt.

"You know this is a total waste of time," she said, looking down at her brother.

Dave ignored her and kept digging.

"Dave, face it," she said. "You'll never be Prom King, and no one will ever swim in this stupid pool."

Stoney laughed, and helped himself to a pastry. "Go easy on him, little weasel. I think he's having a breakdown."

Teena shook her head. "You're wrong, Stoney. He's just desperate." She turned to go back to the house. "Mom says to drink your juice and go to school. Later," she said over her shoulder, not waiting for an answer.

Dave put his shovel down and jumped out of the hole. Then he and Stoney sat on the edge, drinking their juice and chewing their Pop-Tarts.

Boris lay down next to Dave, wagging his tail and waiting for potential crumbs.

"Buddy, stop snappin', man," Stoney said, with his mouth full. "High school's over. We are who we are." He paused, with mock significance. "*Accept* it."

Dave shook his head. "No, I've decided, Stone. I want to look back on my high school career and think, I started slow, but — " he indicated the hole " — I finished strong. I mean, it's almost over, and I've got nothing to show for it."

"Not true, bro," Stoney said cheerfully. "You turned out to be a nine-to-five Dow Jones stern individual, and *I* turned out to be a stoney individual with a crusty mop chillin' on my melon. They're opposites, but they're both cool."

Dave shook his head again, and sighed. "That's not enough. I want more. I want my own page in the yearbook."

Stoney took another Pop-Tart. "Jump off the top of the gym and splatter all over the street. And then, bud, you'll get the *cover*."

Dave smiled, but only a little. "It's not funny, Stone. I'm *not* going down as the geek kid from Encino."

Stoney shrugged again, too busy eating to bother disagreeing.

"When I get this pool finished," Dave said, "I'm going to have *the* killer party after the Prom. I will be Prom King, and graduate a legend. And . . . you'll be there."

Stoney grinned at him wryly. "Robyn is never going to go to the Prom with you. I mean, I wish she would, but she's not."

"Robyn Sweeny is mine," Dave said, not even noticing as Boris snuck a piece of Pop-Tart from his hand. "She's the obvious choice for Prom Queen. She's the most popular, she's become a major babe, and she loves me."

Stoney shook his head. "She finds you crusty, Dave."

"I'll convince her," Dave said, with great conviction. "She'll see the truth."

Stoney looked over at him, his hair flopping in front of his eyes, apparently about to impart a choice piece of skewed Stoney wisdom. "The truth is, dude," he said, "life is about greasing the do back, and weezing on the buffest. High school was an interesting, but harsh ride, and now we are on to bigger and better things."

11

"I *am* on to bigger and better things, Stone," Dave said, and looked very determined. "Count on it."

Stoney took the last Pop-Tart. "If you say so."

"*Count* on it," Dave said.

Chapter 3

After breakfast, Dave and Stoney stopped by Stoney's apartment before going to school. Stoney parked his scooter at the base of a wooden staircase, and Dave looked up at the ratty old building.

"I wish you still lived next door," he said.

Stoney put on a brave grin. "We're chillin' okay."

Dave nodded. "Remember when your dad and my dad used to take us to breakfast on Sunday?"

"Yeah, so our moms could sleep in." Stoney grabbed a bag of groceries off the scooter and started up the stairs. "Those were cool days."

Inside, the apartment was small and dark and hot. They could hear a television blaring in the other room, and Stoney dropped the grocery bag on a cracked Formica table. Feeling uncomfortable, Dave waited outside, talking through the open door as Stoney fed the fish in the small tank in the corner.

"Honey, is that you?" a sad, drawling voice called from the other room. "Did you get the groceries?"

"Fully," Stoney said, sounding extra-cheerful. "Mom, Dave's here, too."

"Hi, David," Stoney's mother called. "How's your mother?"

"Good, Mrs. Brown," Dave called back.

There was an awkward silence, and Stoney finished feeding the fish.

"Mom!" He recapped the little can of food. "I got you Doritos."

"I'm in the middle of Kathie Lee and Regis," his mother said. "Just leave 'em on the table, honey."

Stoney shoved his hands in his pockets, and looked down at the battered linoleum.

"It's lousy that your parents split up, and your dad moved so far away," Dave said, to break the silence.

Stoney nodded. "No kidding, buddy. That's as far as you can go, Fiji."

It was quiet again. Dave stuck his head into the dark apartment and looked around uneasily.

"Come on," he said. "Let's get out of here, man."

"Hey, bud, check out my cat." Stoney pointed. "I got a cat."

Dave nodded, too uncomfortable to look. "Come on, man, we're late. Let's go, okay?"

Stoney frowned, then grabbed the bag of Doritos and opened it. They both took some, and then left without looking back.

The Encino High School parking lot was jam-packed as students, teachers, bicycles, cars, and buses all maneuvered for position. Dave and Stoney rode on Stoney's beat-up Vespa. Stoney drove recklessly down the walkway, dodging other students.

"Hey." Dave nudged him from behind. "There she is."

Robyn Sweeny, Dave's obsession, was getting out of a car with a few other senior girls. All of them gathered up their books and other supplies for the day.

"Hey, Robyn!" Stoney let out a wolf whistle. "Ah-oooo!"

Dave smacked him on the back of the head. "Knock it off, man." He watched wistfully as she walked away from them.

Robyn was a neo-normal, and very pretty, although she seemed somewhat uncomfortable with her looks. In many ways, she was a victim of peer pressure, but there was a genuine sweetness in her smile.

Stoney shook his head. "Dave, you're tattered. She shines you. She *always* shines you."

Dave shrugged, and watched her walk towards the school. "We have history."

"You *had* history," Stoney said. "Pre-freshman history. You could have had her back then, dude."

Dave nodded regretfully. "She hadn't hit babe-hood yet, then."

"Well," Stoney said, "milk does a body good, bro."

16

They both watched as Robyn was overtaken by Matt Wilson. Matt was Dave's worst nightmare. He was handsome, popular — and not a real magnanimous guy. At the moment, he was showing off his beautiful new motorcycle.

Behind Matt were Phil, Bill, and Will, Matt's three baseball buddies, all of whom looked remarkably alike. They locked up *their* motorcycles, and then followed Matt closely.

Ella Chester, Robyn's best friend, ran up to meet the group. Ella was cute — and she knew it. She was Miss Popularity, and surprisingly, her big, teased hairdo was just like a prehistoric cavewoman's wild hair.

Dave scowled as Matt gave Robyn a sloppy kiss, and she laughed, pushing him away.

"Matt Wilson," he said, glowering. "What a jerk. What does she see in that oinker, anyway?"

"Well." Stoney thought for a second. "He's got the buff spikes chillin' on his melon. He's *el capitán* of the baseball team. He has his own personal holding company, full of fundage, and he can weez off it ma — "

" — jor," Dave said glumly, finishing the word for him.

"He's got eighteen-inch bi's. . . ." Stoney looked down at his own arms. "I've got fours."

"Yeah, okay, okay," Dave said. "Fine. But, *besides* that."

"He walks like this" — Stoney demonstrated — "and the nugs fully lose it."

Dave just sighed.

Unfortunately, it was all true.

Jerry Brushe, who taught natural history at Encino High, stood at his desk, trying to get his papers together. Jerry was an archaeology nut in his mid-thirties, who looked like Indiana Jones with love handles. The classroom was filled with strange and bizarre archaeological finds from his many travels. Posters of prehistoric man and dinosaurs lined the walls.

The room was filled with antsy seniors, and even though the bell had already rung, there was complete chaos.

Robyn and Ella were sitting in one corner of the room.

"So, what'd you and Matt do last night?" Ella asked, touching up her mascara.

"We rode around on his motorcycle and watched his friends rip aerials off cars," Robyn said, without much enthusiasm. "*Again.*"

Ella looked away from her compact mirror. "You sound like you didn't like it or something."

"No, I did," Robyn said, not sounding sure at all.

Ella snapped her compact shut. "Don't be stupid. Matt is the dopest guy in school, and he's into *you.* Take advantage of it while you can." She took out several lipsticks, comparing colors before selecting one. "My mom says that most girls peak during their senior year of high school, and it's all downhill from there, so go for it."

"You think so?" Robyn asked doubtfully.

"I *know* it," Ella said. "Don't waste the best year of your life."

Robyn looked uncertain . . . and worried.

"People, people . . ." Jerry said patiently from behind his desk. He motioned with his hands as he tried to get the class to settle down. "Come on, people."

This had no effect.

"I've got some backstage passes for Openhead Wound!" he said. "Anybody interested?"

The class snapped to attention.

"All right then," Jerry said. "Put a lid on it, and take your seats!"

They did.

"Okay," Jerry said, relieved. "Now. Last week we talked about prehistoric man in the . . ."

No one answered.

"Ice Age," Stoney said casually, almost under his breath.

Jerry nodded. "Right. The Ice Age, right! Good, Stoney." He gave Stoney a one-hand snap, which Stoney returned. "Okay," Jerry went on. "So, they called these chunks of ice . . ."

No one said anything.

"Glaciers," Stoney muttered.

"Glaciers!" Jerry agreed. "Right! Come on people, keep up with Mr. Brown here." He winked at Stoney, who was a little embarrassed by all the attention.

The rest of the class looked bored.

"Okay," Jerry said, going back into his lecture. "So, thousands of years ago, glaciers covered the northern hemisphere. As they moved down from the Arctic, they froze the ground ahead of them and created underground ice floes. And check this out, there are some scientists who say that there are still underground glacier movements in *this part of the world*. But, you know what, class? I think that's — "

"Lame!" everyone shouted.

Jerry nodded enthusiastically. "Lame! Right!"

Kim, a brainy student already halfway to MIT, raised his hand.

"Yes, Kim?" Jerry said.

Kim straightened his glasses infinitesimally. "I don't mean to dispute your theory of implausibility," he said, in a measured voice, "but isn't it true that last year, a team of explorers discovered a Neanderthal man completely preserved in the Swiss Alps?"

"Partially preserved," Jerry corrected him. "And he was from the Bronze Age. It's uncommon to discover these kinds of finds, but don't forget, prehistoric glaciers covered most of our continent."

He went over to the chalkboard and pulled down a chart with a picture of a menacing, spear-carrying Neanderthal man. "Okay. . . . Neanderthal man," he said, pointing.

"Whoa," Ella said, from the back of the room. "He's dope. I'd go out with *him*."

Jerry smiled. "Not likely, Ella. Neanderthal men were extremely brutal. Not yet having developed reason or logic, they took whatever they wanted and that, Ms. Chester, included their women."

The more macho and immature guys in the class laughed, and Dave watched in disgust as Matt Wilson grunted and tugged on Ella's hair.

"Barbaric," Ella said, once she had pulled free.

"Indeed," Jerry said vaguely, then looked down at his notes. "Now, where were we?"

The picture of the Neanderthal man looked just like the prehistoric caveman who had been swept away by the avalanche.

Chapter 4

After school, Dave was hard at work on his pool. He had managed to convince Stoney to help him, but Stoney was working significantly less hard. The day had turned into a scorcher, and they were both huffing, and puffing, and covered with dirt.

Boris, the dog, sat by the edge of the ever-deepening hole, watching them, and scratching at the occasional flea.

"So, did you ask her yet?" Stoney asked, stopping to rest, which he did every couple of minutes.

Dave shook his head. "Not yet. Last time

I tried to talk to her, Matt Wilson and his gang of mentals tore off my gym shorts."

"It's hot," Stoney said, resting.

"Yeah." Dave turned in the direction of the house. "Mom! Help!" he bellowed. "We're dying of thirst!"

"Crack that whip, bro," Stoney said.

Dave nodded. "Yup."

A couple of minutes passed, and then Mrs. Morgan came out with some cold sodas. She was friendly and outgoing, and she and Dave had a very playful, bantering relationship.

"David," she said, not unkindly, "when you scream like that, I want to sneak into your room at night and staple your mouth shut."

Dave made a face. "Nice, Mom — like I don't have *enough* things to worry about."

"Remember that the next time you scream." Mrs. Morgan smiled. "Hello, Stanley. How was my last bagel?"

"It was good," Stoney said. "I was hungry."

"I'm sure you were," Mrs. Morgan said, her voice wry.

Stoney stopped digging — again — and

leaned on his shovel. "Mrs. Morgan. I hope you've noticed that your son is fully tattered."

Her nod was long-suffering. "He was *born* fully tattered," she said. "A normal person wouldn't be digging a hole in his parents' backyard and driving everyone insane." She paused. "How's your mother?"

Stoney went back to digging, not quite looking at her. "She's chillin'."

Dave gestured towards the house. "Mom, what's going on inside?"

"Carol's over," Mrs. Morgan said. "We're calling all the district representatives. We're thinking of starting a center for the homeless."

Dave looked around the spacious backyard. "I hope it's not going to be near the house."

"Actually Dave," Mrs. Morgan said brightly, "it's going to be *in* the house. In your room, as a matter of fact."

He lowered his shovel to stare at her. "Mom!"

"Dave!" she said, imitating him. She smiled, and put the cans of soda by the edge of the pool. "Here are your sodas. Don't drink them too fast, you'll get an ice headache." Then she headed back towards the house.

Dave jumped out of the pool, and got the sodas. He and Stoney drank them — too fast, which gave them headaches — and went back to digging.

As the afternoon wore on, Stoney got bored and set up a lawn chair. He lay in it, sunbathing, while he wore his Walkman and played with a yo-yo. Dave doggedly kept digging, going deeper and deeper. Then, his shovel hit something hard, and he stopped.

"Hey," he said.

There was no response from Stoney, who was bopping along as he listened to his Walkman.

"Stone!" he said.

Stoney didn't even look up, so Dave climbed out of the hole, pulled back his earphones, and screamed into his ear.

"Stoney!" he yelled.

Stoney opened his eyes and blinked. "Buddy, chill. My lobes."

Dave grabbed him and pulled him into

the hole. Then, he tried to dig up the hard object, but he couldn't.

"What do you think this is?" he asked, trying to pry it out with his shovel.

Stoney knelt down, and put his hand to the earth. "Feel the ground," he said, and pressed his hand down more firmly. "It's chillin', and not like *chillin'* chillin', but *really* chillin'."

Boris jumped into the pool, sniffing the ground suspiciously. Then, he started growling, and digging with frantic, flailing paws.

"Boris! Easy, dude," Dave said, pulling him away.

They dug out what appeared to be a clump of dirt caked on some kind of round object. Dave grabbed one of Stoney's many scarves and wiped off the caked dirt to reveal the object completely.

It was a prehistoric Mousterian bowl.

Stoney just stared at it, genuinely unable to believe his eyes. "Dude, I know what this is."

"What is it?" Dave asked, a little disappointed that it was just a dumb old bowl.

"It's . . . a Mousterian bowl," Stoney

said, still staring in amazement.

"Get out!" Dave said, then paused. "What's a Mousterian bowl?"

"A *Mousterian bowl*," Stoney repeated, emphasizing the words. "From the Mousterian era?"

Dave looked at him blankly.

"Prehistoric artifacts for 500, Alex," Stoney said, then shook his head, exasperated. "Don't you *ever* watch *Jeopardy*?"

"No," Dave said. "I'd miss *Gilligan's Island*."

"*Tape* Gilligan. *Watch* Jeopardy." Stoney started walking up the ridge of the hole, holding the strange ancient artifact up against the light of the sun to look at it more closely.

As he did, the ground began to shake in another powerful tremor.

"Earthquake!" Dave yelled — unnecessarily.

"Ahhh!" Stoney lost his balance on the moving mound of dirt and fell. The bowl flew out of his hands.

Dave saw it and threw himself stomach-first in the same direction and caught the precious bowl just before it hit the ground and smashed to pieces. When he landed, his body slammed against the surface of the earthen pool floor, but he managed to hold the bowl safely in the air.

"Nice save, Davage," Stoney said admiringly.

The earthen pool floor was cracking open, and Dave came face-to-face with a block of ice.

Then, the tremor ended, and Mrs. Morgan poked her head out the screen door.

"You boys okay?" she called.

"Yeah!" Stoney called back, still lying where he had fallen.

Dave stayed on his stomach, and stared at the block of ice in disbelief. It didn't seem possible, but embedded in that block of ice was . . . a man.

"Stoney?" he said, not quite trusting his voice.

"Yeah?" Stoney answered, flat on his back in the dirt, looking up at the sky.

"It's — " Dave swallowed. "There's a guy buried in my swimming pool."

Chapter 5

They looked at each other, looked at the block of ice, and looked back at each other. Then, they both panicked and scrambled out of the pool, totally freaked out.

They ran towards the house, with Boris following and barking loudly. The sliding glass doors were closed, and Mrs. Morgan was on the telephone. Her friend Carol sat beside her, taking notes. Dave and Stoney banged on the glass doors and yelled at the tops of their lungs, while Mrs. Morgan, still on the phone, shooed them away.

"There's a guy buried in the swimming pool!" Dave yelled.

"Yeah!" Stoney banged on the door. "He's all frozen, and — "

"A *real* guy!" Dave said. "A *dead* guy!"

Mrs. Morgan waved at them to go away, or at least wait for her to finish her call.

"Mom, I'm *serious!*" Dave shouted.

Mrs. Morgan just pulled the curtains closed to shut them out.

Dave and Stoney looked at each other.

"I don't think she believes us," Stoney said.

"Oh, yeah?" Dave banged on the door once more — to no avail. "What gave you that idea?"

Stoney shrugged, and they went back to the edge of the pool, to look in and decide what to do next. The man in the block of ice was like some secret prize they might have found in a Cracker Jack box when they were five. Except, of course, it would have had to have been an extremely *large* box of Cracker Jack.

"You know, they never found Jim Morrison," Stoney said, after a long pause.

"Yeah, and they never found Jimmy Hoffa," Dave agreed.

Stoney nodded. "Or Jimmy Mahoney."

Dave shot him a sharp glance.

"Kid I knew in Cub Scouts," Stoney explained.

Dave started to say something, then decided not to pursue it.

Stoney climbed into the pool. "Dave, I know what it is," he said suddenly.

Dave frowned, and kept his distance. "What?"

"A *caveman*," Stoney said.

Dave laughed, and gave him a smack on the back of the head.

Stoney smacked him back. "No, I'm serious, check it out!"

So, Dave looked again. Beneath the ice, just barely, he could see that the man was holding a spear. A spear!

"Wow," Dave said, and took a cautious step away from the block of ice. "A caveman. Unbelievable. This is *big*, Stone. This is tremendously large. Do you know what this could mean for us? Fame, money — *popularity*."

Stoney shook his head. "Far too much responsibility for me, bud. Anyway, I'm *already* popular."

"Yeah," Dave agreed, "you travel in large crowds of *one*."

Stoney shrugged, not even remotely offended.

"Stone, this is important," Dave said, serious now. "This is my chance to make something of myself. You've got to help me dig him out. You were *here*. You're a part of this."

Stoney shook his head again and got out of the pool. "I don't want to be a part of anything, Dave. I'm happy just to be me."

Dave put his hands on his hips, frustrated. "What if this means money?" he asked. "You couldn't use a new scooter? A new wet suit?" He tried to think of something even better. "A little fundage to attract older nugs with a mansion and a pool?"

Stoney closed his eyes as he imagined all of that. "Ahhh . . ." he said.

Dave pressed his advantage. "Soaking up some rays, watching *all* the *Jeopardy* you want?"

Stoney thought about that, then looked at the man in the block of ice holding the spear.

"Well, buddy," he said, "that spear'll look pretty buff on the wall of the sweat box. Okay." He jumped back in. "Let's dig."

Dave grinned, and they one-hand snapped.

They dug until the block of ice was entirely exposed, and then they tried to lift it out of the hole. A couple of potential hernias later, they stopped and sat on the ice block to rest — and think of a better idea.

They ended up taking apart Dave's old swing set and attaching it to a riding lawnmower, to use as a towline. Dave leaped back into the pool and strapped the hunk of ice with a rope hung over the swing set, as Stoney sat at the controls of the lawnmower.

"More gas!" Dave said, once the rope was tied securely. "Give it more gas!"

Stoney did, and Dave took a snapshot of the scene to record it for posterity, before noticing that the ice block still hadn't budged.

"More!" he yelled.

Stoney floored the gas pedal, and Dave

took another picture before getting behind the humongous chunk of ice to help push it up out of the hole.

"He weighs a *ton*," Dave said, panting from the effort of pushing.

Upstairs, Dave's father, Larry Morgan, was looking out of his bedroom window at the scene in the backyard. Mr. Morgan was a man who was a little on the didactic side, and *completely* on the serious side.

"Larry, come to bed," Mrs. Morgan said.

"Why can't he get this motivated about the garbage, or his homework?" Mr. Morgan asked grumpily.

"Larry . . ." Mrs. Morgan said.

He frowned, but closed the curtains.

Down in the yard, they finally pulled the block of ice out of the pool, and Stoney drove the lawnmower back over to the toolshed, dragging the ice chunk along behind. With a lot of grunting and complaining, they were able to muscle the frozen man up onto a pair of sawhorses in the middle of the shed, so that they would be able to see it more clearly.

Dave lit a small lantern and he and Stoney stood in the flickering glow, admiring their discovery.

"*Cool*," Stoney said.

Dave nodded. "*Totally* cool."

They didn't want to leave their caveman alone, so they decided to spend the night guarding the toolshed. They sat outside, Dave holding a rake, and Stoney clutching a shovel. But, by morning, they had long since fallen asleep, and didn't wake up until Boris came barking over to greet them.

"Quit it, Mom," Dave mumbled, trying to push him away. "I'm getting up."

He opened his eyes, and he and Stoney looked at each other, then bolted into the toolshed, afraid of what they *wouldn't* find.

But the caveman was still there, and still encased in the thick block of ice.

Dave let out a sigh of relief, closing the door behind them. "He's still here."

"No kidding, bro," Stoney said. "He's an ice cube."

Dave nodded. "We gotta *defrost* him."

So, before heading to school, Stoney plugged in a space heater, aiming it directly at the chunk of ice, and Dave set up two blow dryers in a couple of vice grips and turned them on full blast.

"We tell no one about this, do you understand?" he said.

Stoney nodded, then frowned. "Can't I tell Steve Kooser?"

"No!" Dave said. "No one! No one can know! We tell *no one!*"

"No one." Stoney nodded again. "Got it."

Then, as Dave posed in various flattering positions, Stoney recorded the initial stage of the defrosting, in vivid color.

Chapter 6

When they finally got to school, Dave looked around everywhere until he found Robyn. She and Ella were hanging out by their lockers, talking and laughing with a group of other popular kids.

Dave tried to make his way over to her through the crowded hall, then stopped to slick back his hair. He took a deep breath, and walked over towards Robyn's locker. He stopped right in front of her, giving her a big, confident smile.

"Hey," he said.

"Hi, Dave." She turned away, and continued digging through her locker.

"Guess what I found?" Dave said.

Ella glanced over at him. "A life?"

"Funny," Dave said, and took Robyn's arm, ushering her away from Ella and the others so that they could talk privately. "Check this out." He lowered his voice. "I found a *caveman*."

"A caveman?" Robyn said in a normal voice.

"Shhh." Dave put his finger to his mouth. "Not so loud . . ."

Robyn tried not to laugh, without much success. "Dave, I hate to be the one to tell you, but — you're drowning."

"I'm serious," Dave insisted. "I found a real caveman. He's frozen. In my backyard. It's really fierce. Wanna come over after school and see him? I'm only inviting a few people."

"I would," Robyn said politely, "but I've got Prom committee, and . . . I'm really not ready to handle a caveman."

Dave nodded. "I understand."

She gave him a warm, winning smile. "Bye, David," she said, and walked away.

"I love it when she calls me David," he said aloud, watching her go.

"Hello, David," a voice said from behind him, and a hand slammed down onto his shoulder. Then, Matt Wilson grabbed him by the shirt and lifted him up so that they would be nose-to-nose.

"Going somewhere?" Matt asked ominously.

"Yeah," Dave said. "I've got a date with your mom."

Matt was not amused, and strong-armed him down the hall, with his posse of Phil, Bill, and Will hustling over to help.

It didn't take long.

Back in the toolshed, the man in the ice block was still lying on the sawhorse. Water from the ice dripped slowly to the floor. There was an enormous puddle there and, under the relentless heat, the ice was beginning to crack.

Suddenly, the sawhorses gave way, and the caveman fell to the ground. The impact stunned him, and then he sat up stiffly. His hair was matted and dirty, and he was covered with icicles. He looked savage and fierce — and very disoriented. He also looked very cold.

The caveman was just getting his bearings when the door suddenly swung open and Boris the dog made a growling charge for him. The caveman grabbed him by the snout, patted him, and grunted something in a whisper. Boris calmed down and wagged his tail tentatively, sniffing at what he assumed was another animal.

The caveman moved to the door and stood in the sunshine, blinking at the sunlight. He was young, and not very big, but obviously strong. It would not be hard to imagine him ripping off a giant sloth's head for dinner.

He looked at the backyard, the pool hole, and the birds in the trees, making small growls of awe deep in his throat. He shivered again, and then cautiously stepped away from the toolshed, and ventured out into the yard.

At the high school, Matt and his posse were staple-gunning Dave to the Prom bulletin board by his clothes. Gold art paper made up the Prom King's and Queen's crowns, and Dave was nailed up right under the King's crown as though it were on top of his head. There were silver sprinkles all over his face, and he tried to struggle free, but the guys held him down.

"You've been a headache ever since third grade," Matt said, stapling Dave's pants cuff to the wall. "I know about your stupid Prom King fantasy. Forget it. If you were on fire, Robyn wouldn't even cross the street. Anyway, she's *mine*."

"You wish," Dave said, even though he was — at the moment — totally helpless, and should probably just have kept his mouth shut.

"No," Matt said. "*You* wish." He took a marker out of his backpack and wrote *Kick Me* across Dave's forehead. Then, he pulled the fire alarm, and he and the posse laughed and ran away.

Up and down the hall, classroom doors started to open. Everyone filed outside and stopped to stare at Dave hanging from the wall.

"Well," Stoney said, emerging from the crowd and folding his arms across his chest. "I guess you got to be Prom King after all."

"Get me down," Dave said grimly.

Stoney nodded, and moved forward to

help him. Teena peeked her head through the crowd, and cringed at her brother's latest public misadventure.

It was not a pretty sight.

The caveman slipped over Dave's wall, a hunter out of his element. He was panting, and frightened, and still very cold. He saw a little stream of water filling the gutter in the street and crawled over to it, lapping the water with his tongue. It tasted horrible, and he spat it out, gagging.

A garbage truck came rolling down the street and stopped right in front of the caveman. There were four garbage cans on the sidewalk, waiting to be emptied. The caveman stared at the back of the truck, paralyzed with fear as its hydraulic arms dumped the cans into its large, chewing mouth. The sound was terrifying and, to the caveman, the truck looked exactly like a large — and hungry — woolly mammoth.

He jumped up and down, waving his arms and yelling at the beast, afraid that it might eat him. When the machine moved closer, its engine screeching and crushing, the caveman ran away, escaping in the nick of time. This quiet neighborhood was like a jungle to him. He kept running, and hid behind a nearby house.

He leaned against a strange-looking tree with yellow fruit and tried to catch his breath. He was just starting to calm down when he heard a high-pitched roar, and saw a long, tubular serpent coming straight towards him. The serpent was blowing away everything in its path, screaming like the gods themselves.

The caveman screamed back, expecting the furious serpent to blow him into oblivion, and then ran for his life, leaving behind him a confused gardener holding a portable leaf blower.

The caveman tore down the block in a complete panic, then crossed the street and headed back towards the Morgans' house. A Mack truck screeched to a halt, almost hitting him.

"Outta da way!" the driver shouted from a window, gesturing angrily.

The caveman didn't even pause, and continued his headlong flight back to the Morgans' house. Mrs. Morgan drove right by him, but didn't notice anything unusual, and the caveman kept running as fast as he could.

Suburban Encino was just too much for him.

Chapter 7

Over at the high school, Dave was leaning over a water fountain, trying to wash *Kick Me* off his head. Stoney was standing next to him, and Dave took off one of his scarves and wrapped it around his own forehead.

"Dude, you've had a bad day," Stoney said. "It's fifth period. Let's go to the Mountain."

Dave shook his head, the scarf flapping. "Maybe we'd better get back to the toolshed. I'm getting worried. We've got to protect our investment."

"*Your* investment," Stoney reminded him.

"Okay," Dave said, "but what if someone steals him?"

Stoney laughed. "Buddy, he's chillin' in a block of ice the size of a sofa."

Dave shook his head, worried. "Stoney, I'm not kidding. He's a valuable prehistoric artifact!"

"Well, so's my scooter," Stoney pointed out, "and I don't see anyone stealing *that*."

Dave considered that, then nodded. "Good point."

"Let's go to Mega Mountain," Stoney said, and looked around the empty halls, shuddering. "I'm starting to freak on *escuela*, bro."

Dave laughed, and they headed for their next class.

By now, the caveman had found his way inside the Morgans' house . . . and had discovered the kitchen. More importantly, he had discovered the refrigerator.

He grabbed a milk carton and downed most of it, spilling the rest. Then, he saw his Mousterian bowl on the counter, next to some Tupperware bowls. He compared the two, finding that the Tupperware bent, but didn't break.

He liked the Tupperware *much* better.

He wandered into the living room, accidently stepping on the remote control box, which was on the floor. The television snapped on, revealing the Terminator, who was saying, "I'll be back . . ."

The caveman moved closer to the television, taking in the scene, then stepped back and landed on the remote control again, and the station changed to MTV. A Third Reich Headbanger video was just ending, and the next video that came on was Yothu Yindi's Video Treaty.

It looked very primitive, and the caveman moved in time to the music, dancing one of his best caveman dances. He picked up a bowl of candy from the coffee table and dumped the candy out. He turned the bowl over and banged on it like a bongo, pretending it was his old prehistoric log.

By mistake, he danced onto the remote control again, and the channel changed automatically. *The Flintstones* came on, and he cooed and watched. He backed into the recliner and it fell back, flicking into its vibrator mode. The caveman thought he was going to hit the ground, but the chair reclined to a comfortable position. The caveman watched *The Flintstones*, from the vibrating lounger.

He had become the first Neanderthal couch potato.

Dave and Stoney sat in their English class, watching the final seconds tick down from 2:59 to 3:00. When the bell rang, they jumped over desks in their rush to get to the door, and ran out to the parking lot. Stoney had a little trouble getting his scooter started, but then they sped straight to Dave's house.

When they got to the toolshed, the door was open, and there was nothing left inside except an empty pair of sawhorses and a large puddle.

"He melted!" Dave gasped. He stared at the puddle, then fell to his knees in disappointment.

Stoney patted him on the back, trying to console him.

"It wasn't meant to be, little weasel," he said. "Come on, I'll buy you some jerky."

Dave nodded, and they headed for the house. The kitchen was a complete disaster area, looking as though something had exploded in it. Dave and Stoney exchanged shocked glances.

Hearing the television, Dave pointed towards the living room, and they went in there to find the television on and the empty recliner vibrating and tilted backwards. There was candy all over the floor, and caveman drawings on the big screen television.

They surveyed the damage in stunned amazement. They looked at each other, looked around the room, and looked back at each other, both thinking the exact same — terrible — thing.

Then, the smoke alarm at the top of the stairs went off.

"Ahhh!" they both shouted, and ran upstairs. Smoke trailed out from underneath Dave's bedroom door.

"You first," Dave said.

Stoney shook his head. "Your house."

Dave opened the door, and saw that his

room had been transformed into a prehistoric hovel. The bed and shelves had been taken apart, and there was just a big pile of wood and books in the middle of the floor. The caveman was squatting over what had been the furniture and was rubbing two sticks together.

Quickly, Dave shut the door, and he and Stoney looked at each other.

"He's alive," Dave said, barely breathing. "He was practically an ice cube, practically."

"I say we walk," Stoney said. "The liability factor is far too harsh, buddy."

"No way, man," Dave said stubbornly. "No way. He's *ours*."

They opened the door and peeked into the room again. They watched the caveman make himself at home. Quickly, they closed it a second time.

"Be very hospitable," Stoney said.

"I know what I'm doing." Dave slid the door open, and then hesitated. "I think."

He stepped into the room. Stoney saw a catcher's mask on the floor and immediately put it on for protection, staying *behind* Dave every step of the way.

The caveman turned around and, seeing the two strangers, became viciously territorial. They all stared at each other, and the caveman bared his teeth and growled. Dave and Stoney smiled at him like idiots.

"Hey." Dave broadened his smile until he looked like a Welcome Wagon worker. "How you doing?"

The caveman growled.

"Uh, this is my room," Dave said.

The caveman snarled.

"I'm Dave," Dave said, undaunted. "And this is Stoney. We just want to welcome you to Encino. We're really glad to make your acquaintance."

"And we hope you don't rip our throats out," Stoney said, barely audible.

The caveman's growl was now even more menacing.

"We go to high school," Dave said.

Stoney gave him a jab in the side. "He doesn't know what high school is."

"He doesn't know what a room is. He doesn't know what *anything* is," Dave said, keeping on the bright smile. "I'm just talking, Stoney. Trying to keep it calm and easy."

52

Just then, the telephone rang, and the caveman was startled. He grabbed Dave's baseball bat from the floor and held it high above his head.

In response, Dave picked up a skateboard and held it high above *his* head, while Stoney backed into the nearest corner.

The telephone rang, and rang, and rang.

"Answer the stupid phone!" Dave yelled at Stoney, who didn't move.

The caveman threw the bat at the phone, and it finally stopped ringing.

The room was silent, except for Dave's hamster running around and around on his little wheel, going nowhere. The caveman bounced on what was left of the bed with a crazed look in his eyes. His hair stuck up all over the place.

Dave still held the skateboard high above his head, and Stoney now gripped his chest with both hands as though he were considering having a heart attack.

"It's okay," Dave said. "It's okay. I think he's calming down."

But, just as he said that, the caveman let out a loud warrior cry and charged Dave, ready to hunt — and kill.

Chapter 8

Stoney reacted quickly. He stuck his hand in a jar of pennies and other items on Dave's dresser and, just as the caveman was about to bash Dave's head in, he pulled out a Bic lighter and flicked it on.

"Fire!" he yelled.

The caveman stopped to watch, and cooed when he saw the little flame. Stoney held the light out to him like a carrot, and the caveman came closer, forgetting his murderous intentions. Stoney flicked the lighter on and off, and the caveman smiled. As Stoney bobbed the little flame up and down in front of him, the caveman's eyes widened, and he giggled quietly.

"Stone, that was kill," Dave said, lowering the skateboard with still shaking arms.

Stoney gave the caveman the lighter and showed him how to use it. After a few tries, the caveman had mastered this new skill and he flicked the lighter on and watched the flame, absolutely thrilled.

"I don't think he's gonna tweak us anymore, bud," Stoney said, also smiling.

The cavemen took the lighter and bent down to restart his fire.

"No," Dave said quickly. "Oh, no." He snatched the lighter away from the caveman who got mad and picked up the bat again. "*No*," Dave said firmly.

"No," the caveman said in a raspy voice.

There was a moment of stunned silence, and Dave and Stoney looked at each other.

"What?" Dave asked, not sure if he'd heard right.

"I think he just said, *no*," Stoney said, staring at the caveman.

"No," the caveman repeated.

"No!" Dave said.

"No!" Stoney said.

"No!" the caveman shouted, and jumped up and down on Dave's bed, the springs squeaking underneath his weight. "No. No. No. No. No."

Dave and Stoney shook their heads in admiration, marveling at this feat.

"*Cool*," Stoney said, "He's so greasy."

Dave stared at him. " 'So greasy'? He's a prehistoric pyromaniac!" He watched the caveman leap up and down like a maniac. "We're gonna have to teach him stuff."

"Like — how to weez?" Stoney guessed, suggesting his own best skill.

Dave shook his head thoughtfully. "No . . ."

"No . . ." the caveman said from his perch on the bed, mimicking him perfectly.

Dave folded his arms across his chest, and looked over at Stoney. "We have to teach him how to be *normal*," he said.

Stoney made a face. "That's boring, bro. We've got to go psycho with him!"

The caveman kept playing with his Bic lighter, but didn't set anything on fire. While he was distracted by this new toy, Dave and Stoney huddled briefly to discuss the situation, and plan their next move.

"Come on, man," Dave said urgently. "Hang with me. Let's just lay this out. If we call anyone, they'll take all the credit, cut him up into little pieces, and we'll still be geeks."

Stoney looked offended, pulling himself up to his full — limited — height. "I'm not a geek," he said, with great dignity. "I'm a unique weasel. I'm just underrated 'cause I live in Encino."

Dave sighed. *"Bud-dy?"*

It was the ultimate appeal to loyalty.

Stoney looked at the happily bouncing caveman, then let out a resigned breath. "Okay," he said. "You're the boss."

They one-hand snapped to cement the deal.

Now, it was time to get to work.

They enticed the filthy caveman into Dave's parents' whirlpool and then turned on all of the jets full-blast. The caveman jumped up, alarmed by the noisy streams of water, but then decided that he liked the sensation and settled down to enjoy his bath.

Dave opened his mother's cabinet, took

out a bunch of bath salts, beads, and lotions, and poured them all into the tub. Bubbles began to form in the frothy water and the caveman played with them, blowing them onto Stoney and the floor.

While this was going on, Dave looked around for more stuff to put in the tub. He came up with liquid cleanser, toilet bowl cleaner, and scouring powder. As Dave filled the tub with cleaning supplies, Stoney shaved the caveman's body with an electric shaver and splashed some after-shave onto him when he was finished.

The caveman grabbed the bottle of after-shave and tried to drink it.

"No!" Stoney said, tapped his hand gently, and took the bottle away from him.

The second he turned his back, the caveman retrieved the after-shave and drank it, anyway.

When they were finally finished, they led the caveman back to Dave's room and closed the door behind them. Once they had dressed the caveman in *just* the right outfit, they stood back and checked him out. He was all cleaned up, and smelling real fine. In fact, he was just plain awesome.

Stoney picked up the camera, and began recording this transformation.

"He looks buff," Stoney said. "Hey, caveman, can you say buff? Buff?"

"Buff," the caveman said obediently.

Dave gave Stoney a smack. "Stop fooling around. We've got to give him a cool name."

Stoney thought for a second. "How about Axl?"

Dave shook his head in disgust. "Not even," he said. "Don't you understand the importance of this situation? I mean, come on, we've got the Missing Link standing in my bedroom." He stopped. "Link. Link! We could call him *Link*."

Stoney snorted, distinctly unimpressed by this idea. "That's lame."

"Not," Dave said.

"Lame," the caveman contributed. "Not."

From outside in the driveway, they could hear a low grinding sound.

"What was that?" Stoney asked.

Dave shrugged. "Nothing, just the garage door." Then, he stared at Stoney — and Link — in wide-eyed horror. "My parents!"

"Your parents!" Stoney said, equally alarmed.

There was no time to plan, so Dave jumped into action, all of his mental wheels spinning simultaneously. "Okay, okay," he said, trying to stay calm. "Take Link out the back and ring the bell in five minutes."

Stoney looked uneasy. "But — "

"No buts," Dave said. "Do it. Now. And *I'll* do all the talking. Go!"

Stoney shrugged, took the Bic lighter out of his pocket, and flicked it on. "Come on," he said. "Follow the weasel, Linkage."

Dave watched them go, then raced down the stairs towards the kitchen.

He *really* hoped that this was going to work.

Chapter 9

In the living room, Dave turned off the television, put the recliner back in place, picked the candy up off the floor and threw it back in the bowl. He whipped off his T-shirt and used it to clean the caveman drawings from the television screen.

He yanked his T-shirt back on and hurried into the kitchen just as his parents and Teena came in through the back door.

Mrs. Morgan's mouth fell open when she saw the damage. "My kitchen," she said weakly.

Teena smiled, eager to see her brother get in trouble. "Busted," she said, and did her own private one-hand snap.

Mr. Morgan put down his briefcase and paused to survey the messy kitchen. "What are you doing, Dave?" he asked, very calm.

Dave looked very pleased — and self-conscious. "I'm making dinner," he said, and ducked his head in shy embarrassment.

Mrs. Morgan frowned, finding this about as likely as a Cubs/Red Sox World Series. "You're what?"

"*Busted*," Teena said, grinning.

Dave looked hurt. "I'm making dinner," he said. "I thought it'd be a great surprise."

Teena nodded. "They're surprised all right."

The front doorbell started ringing — and didn't stop.

"What is going on around here?" Mr. Morgan asked, annoyed, and went to answer it.

When he opened the door, he saw Stoney trying to get Link to stop pushing the doorbell.

"Hello, Stoney," Mr. Morgan said dryly. "Why is that strange boy ringing our doorbell?"

Dave ran over and embraced Link, putting his arm around him and leading him into the house.

"H-e-l-l-o," Dave said, speaking as though Link were both foreign and deaf. "My-new-friend! Come-meet-your-family!"

Mr. Morgan blinked. "Whose family?"

Boris ran in from the backyard and jumped on Link, who wrestled and played wildly with him as though he were a dog, too. Then, they both ran outside, fighting and growling, and having a great time.

Dave's parents and Teena watched this through the front window, stupefied.

"Dave, who *is* that?" Mrs. Morgan asked, staring at Link as he rolled across the grass.

Dave wracked his brain, trying to come up with an answer. "Who is that?" he asked, stalling for time. "Who is that? That's Linkavitch Chomofsky, Mom."

She frowned. "What?"

He looked at her, seemingly crushed and offended, and pointed an accusing finger out the window. "Linkavitch. Link. Linkavitch Chomofsky! Mom! Come *on*, Mom." When he saw no recognition on her face, he looked at his father. "Dad? Doesn't anyone remember anything I say in this house, *ever*?"

They all looked at him blankly.

"What are you talking about, David?" his father asked, then looked at everyone else in the room for possible explanations. "What is he talking about?"

"Linkavitch Chomofsky!" Dave said. "Our exchange student? I told you months ago. I can't believe this!"

"He's going to help us dig the pool," Stoney piped up.

Dave gave him a "let *me* do the talking" scowl.

Mrs. Morgan looked confused. "Why doesn't any of this strike me as familiar at all?"

"Oh, sure, Mom," Dave said, sounding wounded. "Just conveniently forget about something that was really important to me. I told you *like months ago* that the school was giving college credit for seniors who were willing to house exchange students and learn about their cultures. You said yes." He shook his head as if in a daze. "I can't believe you're taking it back!"

"Well — " Mrs. Morgan bit her lip,

watching Boris and Link playing joyfully together. "I'm not taking it back, but . . ."

Dave brushed away apparent tears, rubbing one hand across his eyes. "I mean," Dave pulled in a deep, shuddering breath, "this was really important to me — and really embarrassing, I might add. I mean, he came all the way here from — " his mind suddenly went blank "from — "

"Estonia!" Stoney said.

"Where?" Dave asked, then recovered himself. "Yeah, that's right, Estonia." He looked at his mother sadly. "And you've totally blown me off — *again*."

"Well, I . . . I don't . . ." Mrs. Morgan looked at her husband for help.

"Dad?" Dave asked, sounding pitiful.

"Mom. Come *on*," Teena said, her hands on her hips. "You're not buying this, are you? Dad?"

"Well." Mr. Morgan thought back. "Maybe I do remember you mentioning something about it. . . ."

Dave nodded, pretending to gulp back a few remaining tears. "See?" he said to his mother.

"You're bogus," Teena said.

Dave winked at her. "*You* are."

"I just don't know." Mrs. Morgan frowned again. "How could we have forgotten about this?"

"Gee, Mom, maybe like the way you forgot to pick me up after the school play in third grade and I sat in the parking lot all night," Dave said. "Or maybe like the way you forgot about sending in the dues for the soccer team in sixth grade, and I — "

"All right, David," Mrs. Morgan cut him off, her voice sharp. "We don't have to wander through the entire family history."

"Hey, yeah," Stoney said, coming up with a memory of his own. "What about the time you lost him at Gator Jump-a-Roo?"

Mr. Morgan narrowed his eyes at him. "Please, Stanley." He turned to Dave. "Where is he going to stay?" His eyes narrowed more. "And why is he attacking the dog?"

"He's going to stay in my room, of course," Dave said. "And he's not attacking the dog, he's, uh, bonding."

Teena made a rather rude sound. "As *if*," she said.

Dave scowled at her. "Shut up."

66

"You shut up," she said.

Mr. Morgan waved his hands, motioning for them to be quiet. "Let's everybody shut up," he said. "I'm tired and I'm hungry and I want dinner. Stanley, I assume you're staying?"

Stanley beamed at him. "You assume correctly, Mr. M."

Mr. Morgan nodded, having expected that. "We practically feed the whole neighborhood," he grumbled, "why not part of Estonia as well?"

Teena watched as Link romped with Boris.

"You know something?" she said, almost to herself. "He's kind of cute. . . ."

Mr. and Mrs. Morgan exchanged concerned glances.

Dave and Stoney one-hand snapped.

Later that night, Dave and Stoney helped a reluctant Link into a pair of cow pajamas, getting him ready for bed. Link was reasonably cooperative, but he didn't look very happy about either the situation or the pajamas.

"I can't believe you told my parents he's

Estonian," Dave said, forcing Link's arm into one of the sleeves.

"*I* can't believe you own such dumb pajamas," Stoney said.

"Let's see how smart this guy really is." Dave looked at Link, sitting quietly on the bed. "Okay. I'm Dave. Me Dave. And this is" — he gestured towards Stoney — "Stoney."

Stoney gave him a little wave.

"Stoney," Dave said. "He Stoney. And you — " He pointed at Link, who promptly grabbed his finger. "Ow! Stop!" Dave yanked free. "Okay, you are Link. Link. You Link." He stepped back. "Okay now, let's see how smart you are. I'm — "

"Dave," Link said.

Dave nodded, pleased. "Excellent. And he's — "

"St-Stoney," Link said, stuttering a little.

"Great," Dave said, nodding. "And you, you are . . ."

Link smiled. "Dave."

Dave shook his head. "No. *You*. You are . . ."

"Buff," Link said happily.

Dave patted him on the back. "That's okay, buddy. You've had a big day."

Link saw the Elle MacPherson poster on the back of Dave's bedroom door, and growled appreciatively.

"Yeah," Dave agreed, also admiring the photo. "She's some Betty."

"Betty," Link said, and he growled. "Mmmmm."

Dave and Stoney both laughed, and Link joined in, even though he had no idea what he was laughing at.

"Link, you've had a big day," Dave said. "But tomorrow, *tomorrow*, we're going to take you someplace really special."

"Taco Bell!" Stoney guessed.

"Not even," Dave said, and put his hands on Link's shoulders, looking him right in the eye. "Congratulations, man. Starting tomorrow, you're a *senior*."

Chapter 10

The next morning at school, Link walked down the hall with Dave and Stoney on either side of him. They strode down the corridors like three of the Magnificent Seven. Link looked definitely def in his surf rock clothes. His hair was tied back in a ponytail, and he filled out his long cow shorts and T-shirt nicely.

More than a few of the other students noticed him as they walked by.

"Stand up straight, Link," Dave whispered.

They passed two very fashionable and pretty girls, who turned to stare.

"Who's that guy with the dork squad?" one of them, Kathleen, asked.

"He's totally rude," the other one, Nora, said.

"Totally," Kathleen agreed, and they both giggled, trying to catch Link's eye.

Down in the attendance office, students were waiting with sick notes and hall passes. The line went all the way out into the corridor. Dave and Stoney waited in the middle of the line, while Link slouched in a chair by the wall, looking remarkably like any other senior with a bad attitude.

"Poor unfortunate weasel," Stoney said, watching him. "He's spent a million years on ice and *now* he has to go to high school."

Dave sighed. "Well, he can't stay at my house anymore — he might eat my sister."

"That'd be cool," Stoney said

Dave grinned, but let that pass. "Look, we've got a real find here," he said. "This guy is our key to popularity and fame. We'll get him enrolled, he'll help us get cool, and we'll help him get famous." He looked over at Link, who was scratching enthusiastically. "We'll teach him a few stupid pet tricks and call Letterman."

Stoney shook his head. "Come on, buddy, that's like, harsh. You're weezing off his gig."

"Oh, please, he's a *caveman*," Dave said. "Practically a monkey. We found him. We can do whatever we want with him."

" 'We-we-we,' " Stoney said. "No, buddy, it's you-you-you, dude. I'm chillin' solo on this one."

Dave frowned, but he didn't argue.

When they got to the front of the line, Dave brought Link over to Mrs. Mackey, the very old, blue-haired attendance lady.

Mrs. Mackey lifted her glasses from the chain around her neck to squint at Link. "And what do we have here?"

"Uh, Linkavitch" — Dave tried to remember — "Chomofsky. He's from Estonia."

Mrs. Mackey squinted her eyes some more. "It's a little late in the school year, don't you think?"

"Not for Estonians," Dave said without hesitation. "This is when they *start* their school year."

"I see." Mrs. Mackey felt for her glasses,

realized that she already had them on, and
fluttered her eyes a few times to focus.
"Transcripts, please?"

"Uh, we don't, uh . . . that is — " Stoney
stopped, trying to think of a good excuse.

"His bags haven't cleared customs,"
Dave explained.

Margot, a very beautiful, dark-haired
senior, walked by and Link turned to ogle
her.

"Grrr," he said. "Betty."

Margot stopped, flattered. "No, Margot.
Do I know you? Have we met?"

"We met," Link repeated.

"Oh," she said, looked at him for a long
minute, and then left.

Mrs. Mackey was still very concerned
about the lack of transcripts and Link's
other Estonian school records. "Well, when
will they arrive?" she asked.

"Soon," Dave promised. "Soon."

Mrs. Mackey moved her squint away
from him, and towards Link. "What is your
name?" she asked him.

"Dave," Link said.

Mrs. Mackey peered through her glasses

down at her enrollment form, and then peered at Dave. "I thought you said his name was Linkavitch?"

Dave nodded, thinking quickly. "Dave is his nickname."

Mrs. Mackey was finding all of this a little hard to comprehend, but she gave Link several forms to fill out, and a pen. "If you don't have any records, he'll have to fill out an SC-480," she said. "I'll assign him to your classes, since he's staying with you. I assume he'll want driver's ed." She shuddered. "They always do."

Dave took the forms before Link could start scribbling cave drawings on them, not even wanting to *think* about the possibility of Link behind the wheel of a car.

Once the forms were completed, Dave and Stoney walked Link towards their first class. Link ran his hands along the cool metal of the lockers and played with the combinations, opening more than one by mistake.

"Stop that," Dave said.

"Stop that," Link repeated, but kept on doing it. Then, he saw Robyn and Ella standing by their lockers and sniffed in their general direction, looking excited.

"What's he doing?" Stoney asked.

"I don't know," Dave said uneasily. "Maybe this wasn't such a good idea after all."

Link walked over to the two girls, and sniffed. It was Ella's perfume that he smelled, and he moved closer, smelling her strangely familiar-looking surfer-chick prehistoric hair.

"Excuse me," Ella said, edging away.

Not knowing what that meant, Link kept sniffing.

Ella slapped him. "Hey, cool it, *amigo*!"

Link backed her up against a locker, sniffing.

"Wow," Ella said, overcome by his primal reaction. "Is this dude totally fundamental, or what?"

Robyn just stood there with her mouth agape.

"Hey, Link," Dave said, and tapped him on the shoulder. "*No.*"

Link stopped immediately and stood at Dave's side like a good puppy.

"So." Dave gave Robyn his best suave smile. "You miss me?"

Robyn opened her locker and took out her books. "Always."

"This is Link," Dave said. "He's . . . he's from Estonia."

Link shifted his weight, and played with the zipper on his jacket.

"*Cool*," Ella said, checking him out.

"Yeah," Dave agreed, "He's, uh, staying with us for a while."

For the first time, Ella noticed who Link was with. "You're kidding," she said. "This guy? Staying with *you* guys?"

Link grunted a little and touched Robyn's hair.

"He's thinking of becoming a hairstylist," Dave said.

Stoney nodded, and shook his own hair. "Designing crusty mops for the rich and famous.

"Grrr," Link said, and Ella and Robyn both smiled.

Their first class was Jerry Brushe's natural history class. Seeing the blackboard, Link trotted over and picked up a piece of chalk. Then, he began drawing caveman drawings on the board. He knocked an eraser over and it fell to the floor, chalk dust flying. He retrieved the eraser, grabbed another one, and began pounding them together in a tribal sort of rhythm. The chalk dust formed a cloud around his head.

Dave and Stoney just looked at each other and shook their heads.

Matt Wilson and his posse, sitting in the back of the room, pointed at Link and laughed.

"Who is this idiot, anyway?" Matt asked.

Ella turned around in her chair. "His name is Link. He's from Estonia, and *I* think he's dope."

"Yeah?" Matt looked dubious. "You do?"

"Yeah," Ella said. "And I'm not the only one. I think it's great we finally have some new blood around here."

Matt looked at Robyn. "What do you think?"

Robyn's shrug was maybe a little too casual. "He's all right," she said, "if you like that kind of musky animal magnetism."

Before Matt had a chance to respond to that, Jerry came into the room to start class.

"Hey, man, that's excellent work," he said, when he saw Link's cave drawings. Then, he paused. "Who are you?"

Link didn't answer, intent on completing his depiction of a mammoth hunt.

"I said," Jerry raised his voice, "who are you?"

"Betty," Link said.

Jerry tilted his head in confusion. "Excuse me?"

Dave walked over to Link, patting him on the shoulder. "That's Estonian for 'good morning, sir,' " he said.

Link smiled, and nodded.

"Oh. Well." Jerry also smiled. "Right back at you! High-five, man!" He put his hand up for Link to slap, which Link did — *hard*. Jerry pulled his hand back, wincing slightly, then showed it to Kim, the future MIT student who was sitting in the front row. "Did he take any skin off?" Without waiting for an answer, he glanced back at the eerily accurate cave drawings.

There was definitely something odd about this new student. He just wasn't quite sure what it was.

Chapter 11

After class, Dave turned the responsibility for Link over to Stoney for a while.

"Catch you next period," he said. "Watch him."

Stoney nodded, although Link was already wandering away down the hall towards a group of kids who were dancing to the sounds of a beat box. Link barged right into the elite circle, pressing his hand to the beat box. It was too loud, but he started moving in time to the music, dancing his caveman dance. The other kids watched, and then joined in, trying to pick up the new steps.

"Uh, Link, we've got Spanish," Stoney said, from the sidelines. "Señorita Vasquez awaits."

Link was too busy dancing to hear him.

"Link, *Spanish*," Stoney said. "*Taco. Guacamole. Salsa.* Chips." He grabbed Link's arm and dragged him down the hall, still dancing.

The Spanish class took place in the language lab, and Link sat in the little glass booth next to Stoney's, his earphones perched precariously on his head. *Restaurant Phrases* was written across the blackboard, and everyone in the class was repeating what was being said to them.

"*El queso está viejo y podrido,*" Señorita Vasquez said, which meant, "The cheese is old and moldy."

"*El queso está viejo y podrido,*" the class repeated.

"*El queso está viejo y podrido, dónde está el sanitario?*" Señorita Vasquez recited, which meant "The cheese is old and moldy, where is the bathroom?"

"*El queso está viejo y podrido, dónde está el sanitario?*" the class said.

Link repeated each Spanish phrase in turn, looking around his booth, feeling the glass with both hands, and then licking it.

Unexpectedly, Ella dragged her chair over to sit next to him.

"You're cute," she whispered, taking off his earphones.

"You're cute," Link said.

Ella smiled. "Meet me at Blades tonight."

"Blades tonight," Link recited.

"Good." Ella turned to Stoney. "You guys can just, like, drop him off in front or something, right?"

"Uh, sure," Stoney said, and looked at Link a little enviously.

Ella winked at Link, who winked back.

After school, Stoney took Link to the Seven Food Mart, which was run by two guys named Rajnish and Kashmir. Stoney steered Link up and down the aisles, filling his arms with an array of junk food.

"Rajnish, dude," Stoney called up front, "how long for the burrito?"

"Two minutes," Rajnish said.

"*One* minute," Kashmir said.

Stoney grabbed a bag of Oreos and tossed them at Link.

"Linkage, now listen," he said. "I know you were used to eating twigs and stuff, but we've got something called the four basic food groups." He picked up a package of Milk Duds. "Okay, dairy. Milk Duds. You hide these under your pillow so your mom won't snake 'em." He grabbed a roll of Sweet Tarts from another shelf. "Fruit group. Vegetable group — Corn Nuts . . ."

Up front, a microwave bell went off.

"Cool, buddy — the meat group!" Stoney led Link over to the microwave and took out their burrito.

Link snatched it out of his hand, but Stoney shook his head.

"Link, equals," he said, and split it in half.

Link gobbled his half down, but Stoney took only one bite of his.

"Figures," he said. "Hot on the outside, icy in the middle." He looked at Link, who was already finished with his. "You're into that, aren't you, dude? Cool." He handed Link the rest of his to finish.

Link gulped down the burrito half in two bites.

"One time," Stoney said conversationally, "I was riding my scooter, and the same thing happened. I got so edged that I Howarded it and it hit some dude's windshield with Illinois plates. The guy snapped into his own Nam. 'What's this burrito on the windshield. It smeared and I'm just trying to make my way to Disneyland.' "

He stopped to wait for Link's reaction, but Link just stared at him, expressionless.

"Well," Stoney said. "I guess you had to be there."

He went over to the Icey machine, and Link followed him, opening packages and stuffing food into his mouth along the way.

"And for our beverage? The Icey." Stoney stuck his head under the Icey machine and hit the button. Slushy goo slid into his open mouth.

"No, no!" Rajnish shouted. "Stop!"

"You cannot do this!" Kashmir said, grabbing the food from Link, and pushing Stoney aside. "You must leave now. Now, you must leave, please."

"Rajnish, Kashmir, chill, bud-dies,"

Stoney said. "We were just weezing some juice for our trip to the Mountain."

Rajnish shook his head firmly. "No weezing the juice."

Link wandered over to the Icey machine. "Weez the juice," he said softly.

Stoney looked at Rajnish and Kashmir. "Okay, buds, chill," he said.

Kashmir glared at him. "No buds chill."

"Mr. Stoney, you leave now," Rajnish said.

"*Good-bye,*" Kashmir said.

Stoney nodded and turned to get Link — who now had his head under the Icey machine, and was sucking up goo. Stoney grabbed him and they ran out of the food mart, laughing. Then, Link stuck his head back in the store.

"I'll be back," he said in a Terminator voice, and he and Stoney both cracked up.

They rode Stoney's scooter over to Mega Mountain, and Stoney took out his camcorder to record Link's first trip to the amusement park.

He turned the camera on, holding it far enough away to film himself.

"This is Linkage's and my trip to the mountain," he said into the lens. "Come on, Link."

Link moved into the camera frame, and Stoney slung an arm around him.

"Link, say hi," he said. "I'm a weasel!"

Link looked straight into the camera lens. "Hi. I'm a weasel!"

"Cool!" Stoney said, and led him into the park.

While they waited to go on the roller coaster, Link filmed Stoney for a while.

"Buddy, you've been chillin' in an ice cube for so long, you'll need protection." Stoney took two tubes of Day-Glo zinc oxide sunblock out of his pocket, and put Day-Glo green on Link's nose and Day-Glo orange on his own.

Above them, the roller coaster did a loop dee loop.

"The roller coaster is fully harsh," Stoney said cheerfully. "I once saw a guy puke his guts out on the top, and get nailed by it at the bottom." He shook his head. "His furnace was fully tweaked. Well. Let's get on line!"

They rode the roller coaster *fully*, filming each other and digging it, *major*. They went from there to the Freefall ride, where Stoney strapped Link in.

"Okay, Link, are you ready?" he asked.

"Ready!" Link said.

Stoney gave the ride operator a thumbs-up and they were dropped straight down, yelling their heads off and having a great time.

They rode a giant tractor tire through man-made rapids, surrounded by cute chicks in bikini tops and shorts.

"Betty! Betty!" Link said, zooming the camera lens in on them.

"No, buddy," Stoney corrected him. "Fresh nugs!"

"Fresh nugs!" Link said, and splashed water at him.

The girls joined the wicked water fight. Everyone took turns filming the scene. Then, they went to the picture booth and had T-shirts made. Stoney had his face superimposed on a caveman body, and Link had his imposed on a beautiful girl.

"Betty," he said happily.

Stoney laughed. "It's *you*, buddy."

From start to finish, it was a great afternoon.

Dave was sitting on his front steps when Stoney and Link finally drove up on the scooter. When he saw them, he jumped up, furious.

"Where were you!" he yelled at Stoney. "You, like, just split after school! Did you know how worried I was?"

Stoney climbed off the scooter, wincing. "You sound like my mom."

"Not funny." Dave looked from one to the other. "Where'd you get those T-shirts? No, don't tell me, I don't want to know." He pointed at Link. "He's a valuable investment. You have to be careful with him." He frowned, and looked at Link more closely. "What's on his nose?"

"Chill, Dave," Stoney said. "Link and I had a stoney time at the Mountain."

Dave's eyes widened. "You took him to Mega Mountain?"

"Yeah." Stoney grinned. "They're running the roller coaster in reverse."

Dave looked interested for a minute. "They are?"

Stoney nodded, grinned again, and held his stomach.

"Weezing the juice," Link remarked to no one in particular. "Fresh nugs. Check out my cat."

"Oh, no, Stoney!" Dave said with a groan. "Now you've got him talking like you!"

Stoney shrugged. "So?"

Dave slowed down for a minute, and took a deep breath. "Look, Stone," he said, keeping his voice calm. "You've got to be careful with Link. We're getting into Blades tonight because of him. He's *valuable*. Just be careful, okay?"

Stoney shrugged again, not sure why Dave was so concerned. "Okay. Don't be so harsh, buddy."

Link parked the scooter, came over to pat each of them on the back, and then they went inside for dinner.

After they sat down, Mrs. Morgan got up and tucked a napkin into Link's T-shirt before going into the kitchen to bring out their meal. Link squirted some liquid margarine into his mouth, and then burped loudly.

"Excuse *me*," Teena said, disgusted.

"Excuse me," Link repeated, then picked up his silverware and started playing with it, using the small knife as a spear.

Dave took the knife away from him, and showed him how to use a fork. At the same time, Mr. Morgan was staring at Stoney.

"So, Stanley, how's your mother been?" he asked.

"Really bummed," Stoney said. "Can you pass the peas, please?"

"Sure." Mr. Morgan passed him the peas and kept looking at him.

Stoney started to help himself, then stopped.

"Are you guys freakin' 'cause I'm weezing on your grindage?" he asked. " 'Cause if I had the whole Brady Bunch thing going at my pad, I'd be mellow, so don't get edged at my gig, cool?"

Mr. Morgan leaned across the table towards him. *"English,"* he said, enunciating clearly. "Speak English!"

"Dad!" Dave protested.

"Dad!" Link said, mimicking him. Then, he took a box of Milk Duds out of his pocket and sprinkled them all over his plate.

Mr. Morgan shrugged defensively. "What did I do? I can't help it if I never understand him!"

Mrs. Morgan came in with the main dish, and gave her husband a kick underneath the table. "Stanley, you know you're welcome here," she said. "Anytime."

Stoney smiled at Mr. Morgan, who sneered back.

"So," Mrs. Morgan said, changing the subject as she dished out dinner. "How was school?"

"Thrilling," Teena said. "Yesterday, Matt Wilson tacked Dave up to the bulletin board in the hallway."

Dave flushed. "Stall out on the noise, will you?"

"Teena!" Mr. Morgan said, then looked at Dave. "Someone tacked you up to a bulletin board?"

"No," Dave said.

"*Yes*," Teena said.

Dave shrugged, and hunched over his plate. "Dad, I can handle it."

Teena laughed. "In your dreams, Tarzan."

"Talk to me after puberty, braless,"

90

Dave said, and Teena threw some peas at him.

"Stop!" Mr. Morgan said, raising his hands. "Please!"

Mrs. Morgan interceded. "All right, everybody, just relax," she said. "What about Link? How was his day? How is he adjusting?"

Just as she said that, Link saw a fly buzzing around his face. He tried to follow it with his eyes, then used his whole head.

"Good," Dave said. "He's made a lot of new friends."

"As *if*," Teena scoffed.

Link got up, and began stalking the fly. He ended up right behind Mr. Morgan.

"What's he doing?" Mr. Morgan asked, trying to turn and see.

The whole family watched as Link grabbed the fly out of the air and popped it into his mouth.

There was a long silence.

"You need some salt with that?" Teena asked.

Chapter 12

When the meal was over, and Dave had bullied Teena into doing the dishes, he and Stoney drove Link over to Blades, the Encino hangout for the "cool" kids.

"Blades," Dave said wistfully, leaning against the side of his old beat-up AMC Matador. "How cool are we, Stoney? *Finally* part of the elite."

"If we walk in there, the elite are going to beat us up," Stoney said.

Link, drawn by the sounds of music, had wandered over to the front door of the arcade.

"Hey, Link!" Dave shouted after him. "Wait up!"

Link had already gone inside.

Blades was a happening place — a cool half-arcade, half-ice-skating rink, where kids could eat junk food and hang out listening to good music. Everybody who was anybody at Encino High was there, and making lots of noise. Matt and his posse were out on the ice, playing a rough game of hockey.

Link stood at the door, bewildered by all of the activity.

Ella saw him, and came over, holding her arms out to greet him.

"Link! Hey!" She gave him a big hug.

Link was very pleased to see her, and he threw her high into the air and then caught her.

"I'm so glad to see you!" Ella said, having to shout over the noise.

"Glad to see you!" Link said.

Dave and Stoney came rushing in and all of the frantic social activity instantly stopped. Everyone stared at them in complete silence.

Taylor and Boog, two skateboarders,

cruised over to check out these two interlopers.

"Hummer patrol," Taylor said.

"Barneys incoming," Boog said.

"Got 'em," Taylor said.

"Hon, lose the geek squad," Ella whispered to Link. "They're bad for your deal." She led him over to a private area and sat next to him.

Meanwhile, Taylor and Boog smiled at each other. Boog tipped his skateboard so that it rolled right under Dave's feet, and sent him flying straight into Robyn, who was going by.

"Ow!" she said. "What's the matter with you?"

Dave looked sheepish. "Sorry."

Over in the seating area, Ella sat very close to Link, and he ran his fingers through her hair. It was so reminiscent of something . . . something prehistoric. The vague memory made him sad and he dropped his arm, sighing.

"You are like the cutest guy," Ella said, and tried to kiss him.

Link was going to kiss back when his face

clouded over. The vague memory of someone else tugged at his mind, and he pulled
away.

"What's the matter?" Ella asked. "What
did I do?"

Link patted her gently on the head.
"Betty," he said, and sighed.

Stoney hung around next to the kitchen,
where Amy, a waitress, was emptying
glasses and plates. He had a thing for Amy,
who was a large pretty girl just out of high
school and now working her way through
college.

"So, Am-y," he said. "You like swimming?"

She smiled briefly. "I'm kind of busy
right now, Stoney."

He followed her. "Haven't seen you since
you graduated."

"Well, college and stuff," she said.

He nodded. "So, Am-y, you like swimming?"

Now she stopped. "Why, Stoney?"

" 'Cause my buddy Dave's digging a
pool," he said. "We're having a party. It's
going to be buff. There'll be a barbecue,

we've got this caveman — come on, Am-y. It's gonna be cool."

She looked at him as if he were crazy, but she still smiled. "Well, we'll see."

Stoney grinned.

Boog and Taylor skateboarded up.

"Can we get a soda — *please*?" Taylor said, more than a little bossy.

Amy nodded, and hurried off to get his soda.

Stoney frowned at Taylor. "Don't harsh my gig, buddy."

"You're kickin' some crazy flavors, dude," Taylor said. "Busting for a jack move, major."

He and Boog laughed wildly, and skateboarded away.

"Speak English," Stoney muttered after them.

Sitting with Ella, Link was making finger paintings on the table, using ketchup and mustard.

"You're like, so artistic," Ella breathed. She watched as the figure of a woman took shape. "Wow. Is that me?"

"Betty," Link said.

"Oh, *I* get it," Ella said. "Was she like your old girlfriend in Estonia or something?"

Link just sighed.

"Do you miss her?" Ella asked sympathetically. "Well, I can tell you from experience that long distance relationships never work out. Come here."

She tried to kiss him again, but Link just looked at the picture he had drawn, and sighed deeply.

"Estonia's a long ways away, Link," Ella said. "*I'm* right here. Let's work on changing your mind." She tried to kiss him, but he just patted her on the head. "Or not," she said, uncertainly.

Link sighed.

In the meantime, Dave had pulled Robyn into a corner, where he showed her a color snapshot of the two of them, six years old, splashing in a bathtub.

"Don't forget," he said. "We've been naked together."

"And you had *such* a great body then,

97

too." Robyn smiled, putting the picture in her pocket. "I can't believe you still have this."

"My mom found it." Dave let out his breath. "Anyway, look, if you don't think I'm cool, I know you think Link's cool and he's my friend, so that means *I* must be cool, right?"

Robyn looked out at the ice rink. "Dave, you're becoming a pest."

"No, see, I don't think I'm getting through," he said. "Look, you know you love me. You just think I'm bad for your act."

Robyn nodded wryly. "And you think I'm *good* for yours."

From out on the ice, Matt saw Dave and Robyn huddled together. He scowled, bashed some guy away from him, and started skating towards them.

Link walked around, with Ella right on his heels. He saw a video game called Rad Mobile, and stopped to watch. It was the kind a person had to sit inside to play, and the boy already in there was playing with great skill, driving down the video freeway at warp speed.

Link watched, transfixed.

Off the ice now, Matt strode over to Dave and Robyn and pulled them apart.

"What are you doing?" he asked, giving Dave a hard shove. "You're not allowed in here."

"You mean, here, like in the 'here and now'?" Dave asked, pretending to be perplexed. "Or here, as in the greater, existential 'here'?"

Matt motioned for his posse to come over, and they dragged Dave out onto the ice to take care of him once and for all.

Link had finally gotten his turn on Rad Mobile, and he was playing with fierce intensity. A crowd had gathered to watch, and when he crashed and the game stopped, he pounded on the steering wheel in frustration.

"Sorry," Stoney said. "I'm low on fundage, bro."

Link looked around to see if anyone else had a quarter, but then saw Matt manhandling Dave and he scrambled out of the Rad Mobile seat and fought his way through the crowd to get to them.

Out on the ice, things did not look good. Matt and his posse had surrounded Dave, skating in a circle around him, like a *Rollerball Part II* nightmare.

"Are you deaf, dork?" Matt asked. "Didn't I forbid you to speak to her?"

Matt was just about to take a swing at him. Dave closed his eyes and braced himself. Then, hearing a low, threatening growl, he opened them.

"Check out my cat. . . ." Link growled. He had come to the rescue.

Chapter 13

Matt took his attention off Dave and focused on Link. "You want some, too?" he asked, scowling.

Dave grinned, ready to enjoy the sight of Link taking Matt on and pounding him into the ice. Almost everyone from inside the arcade had also gathered around to see what was going to happen — and if there would be blood.

Matt skated over, moving closer until he was right in Link's face, jutting his chin out aggressively.

"I don't know you," he said. "I don't like you, and as of now, I am all over you."

Then, suddenly, he hauled off and punched Link right in the face.

Link reeled, but didn't fall — and didn't hit back.

"Did you see that?" Taylor, one of the skateboard boys, said with great admiration.

"The new kid *took* it!" his friend Boog said, very impressed. "Stayed *up*!"

Pretending that his hand didn't hurt, Matt smirked over his shoulder at Dave. "What do you think of your foreign exchange dork bud now?" he asked, and walked into the crowd, grabbing Robyn's arm. "Let's go. The stench of losers around here is doing damage to my sinuses."

Robyn tried to pull free. "Forget it, Matt. Just don't even come near me! And take this — I don't want it anymore."

"Hey!" He yanked her closer. "Watch it!"

Robyn took his class ring off her finger and threw it as hard as she could onto the ice. Matt bent down and picked it up, trying to hand the ring back to her, but Robyn just stormed off. She pushed through the crowd, stopping when she saw Ella.

"You want him?" she asked, indicating Matt. "He's yours."

As Robyn angrily left, everyone else just stood there without speaking. The crowd seemed divided, but most of them were concerned about Link. Ella, in the meantime, had decided to take Robyn up on her kind offer, and she moved to stand next to Matt, tucking her arm through his.

"All right, show's over," Matt said. "Let's go."

Nobody moved.

Matt raised his voice. "I said, show's over! Get out of here!"

"Matt, are you okay, honey?" Ella asked, snuggling up against him.

The crowd broke up as kids reluctantly began to disperse. Dave and Stoney held a napkin over Link's bleeding lip as they walked him outside to the car.

"I can't believe he got nailed," Dave grumbled. "He's a caveman!"

"He's a pacifist," Stoney said.

"A pacifist caveman?" Dave shook his head. "You're mental."

Link took his T-shirt off and held it

against his lip. There was quite a lot of blood.

"Cavemen aren't like us, Dave," Stoney said, assuming a mock professorial demeanor. "They fought for food and survival, not for popularity. Why should Linkage have hit Matt? What would he be fighting for?"

Dave kicked at the asphalt with one foot. "For face," he said grumpily. "For us. To be *cool*."

Stoney shook his head. "Link doesn't know what cool is. He doesn't even know *where* he is, Dave!"

"Yeah, well," Dave opened the door on the passenger's side of the car, "he's got to learn how to defend himself."

"Against what?" Stoney asked.

"Against jerks like Matt," Dave said, very grim.

He waited as Stoney helped Link into the car, and then closed the door behind them. Link might be a caveman, but it was time for him to start *acting* like one.

When they got to Dave's house, Dave took Link into the living room and turned on the television. First, he put on an old wrestling movie, and he and Link copied the fast-footed moves.

When Dave figured Link had that down, he switched to a karate show, and he and Link tumbled around the room, breaking stuff with their heads and knocking each other down. Stoney lay on the couch watching them, half appalled and half in hysterics.

Next, they watched a black-and-white boxing movie, where the boxer was running in the center of the ring with his arms held up in triumph.

"Yo, Adrian!" Dave shouted, running around the room with his arms above his head.

"Yo, Adrian!" Link yelled in perfect imitation. Then he flipped Dave over his shoulder and pinned him to the floor.

"I think I liked him better as a pacifist," Stoney said.

Dave got up, brushing himself off. "Yeah, but pacifists are lame. The meek never inherit the earth."

He tried to take Link down, but he couldn't. Link picked him up over his shoulders, tossed him onto the couch, and laughed when he landed on top of Stoney.

"Yo, Adrian!" Link yelled, and he and Dave one-hand snapped.

Stoney just groaned.

As soon as they walked into school the next morning, Link was surrounded by cute girls. Ella, however, walked by with her nose up in the air.

"Are you okay?" one of the girls, Kathleen, asked. "We heard Matt clocked you pretty hard."

"Pretty hard," Link said, his ponytail bouncing as he nodded.

"Everybody's talking about it," Kathleen said. "We're all on your side."

A bunch of guys on skateboards, including Boog and Taylor, came rolling over.

"Dude!" Taylor said, holding his fist up in respect. "You took it from Wilson."

Boog nodded, doing a quick spin on his board. "Nobody's ever done that, and survived," he said.

The skateboarders one-hand snapped with Link. Taylor and Boog had set up a ramp outside the front entrance for practicing skateboarding tricks, and Taylor handed Link his skateboard to give it a try.

Link was, of course, a natural, and the skateboarders applauded each and every one of his daring new feats, before trying them out for themselves.

The caveman was a hit.

Chapter 14

In biology class, Dave and Link teamed up together to dissect a frog. Just as Dave was getting ready to make the first incision, Link picked up the frog and popped it into his mouth, whole. Dave quickly opened Link's mouth and took it out, hoping that no one else had noticed.

A pretty girl sitting nearby *had* noticed, but her only reaction was to look at Link and smile, and offer him her frog instead.

At lunch, Link sat at a table surrounded by a few dozen cute girls, including Kathleen and Nora. He had a napkin tucked into his shirt as a sort of bib, and Nora and Kathleen took turns feeding him.

Dave and Stoney, sitting down near the end of the table with none of the girls paying the slightest bit of attention to them, fed themselves.

During art class, Link sat at the pottery wheel, making Mousterian bowls. Even the teacher stopped his lecture to observe, and admire, his new student's work.

Link stayed at the wheel all period long, making history.

At the computer club meeting, Kim and the rest of the club members gathered eagerly around Link as he used a computer mouse to draw caveman graphics.

The computer club members were suitably impressed, and took extensive notes.

That night, at Blades, Link spent the entire time playing Rad Mobile, with a large audience watching. His name was the only one on the scoreboard, and he had become the undisputed champion of the game.

Dave and Stoney smiled as the crowd cheered Link on. Their friend was a complete social success.

Walking into school the next morning, Link was, once again, greeted by everyone in sight, while Dave and Stoney were ignored. Charlie and Peyton, two of the *very* cool kids, stopped to exchange greetings — and high fives — with the new sensation.

"Homeslice!" Charlie said.

Link returned the high five. "Slicey!"

Peyton gave him a clap on the back. "Catch you in Mr. Albert's class, man."

Kim came over to the group, very shy about interrupting. "We, uh, we took a vote, Link," he said. "The computer club feels your presence would be a valuable asset to our organization."

Charlie and Peyton laughed, and made fun of him, each taking a pen from his pocket protector for a souvenir.

Link slung his arm around Kim's shoulder. "Homeboy," he said solemnly.

Charlie and Peyton stepped back, awed by Link's insight, and then returned Kim's pens.

Down the hall, Dave and Stoney watched this scene, both impressed and slightly jealous.

"Why doesn't this ever happen when Matt hits *me*?" Dave asked.

"I don't know," Stoney said, and grinned. "Give yourself a few million years."

That afternoon, Jerry took his senior class to the Museum of Natural History for a field trip. Everyone was there, including Dave, Stoney, Matt, Robyn, and Ella.

"Okay, people," Jerry said. "Follow me and pay close attention to the dioramas."

Link stood in front of a large model of a dinosaur and looked it up and down. He wasn't sure why it made him feel so uneasy. He stared at the first diorama, a scene that looked just like his prehistoric home — not sure why it seemed so familiar.

"I bet none of you knew this," Jerry said, standing in front of one of the dioramas, "but if you took a Neanderthal man, cleaned him up, put him in a suit and rode the bus — say, right next to him — you wouldn't even look at him twice."

As Jerry walked down the long hallway, pausing by each diorama to tell a prehistoric story, Link lagged behind a little. He was having trouble taking all of this in. He recognized what he was seeing, but he couldn't quite put it together with anything in his memory. All he knew was that he felt — strange.

"We are about to witness lifelike examples of the Ice Age, and the end for some Neanderthal men," Jerry said as they turned a corner. "Follow me, people, and pay close attention."

Link lagged further behind the group, going on a tour of his own. He walked along, following the Progression of Man. He saw Man as a primate, Man as a Neanderthal, and Man as he is today. All of this was very disturbing, and Link backed away from the exhibits.

He turned around, only to slam into a plate glass window, behind which a bunch of scientists were constructing a skeletal man. They picked up a foot, and then a hand, before dusting off the skull. Link cocked his head, trying to understand all of this.

He backed away and around the corner, running right into an exhibit whimsically entitled "Valley Girl." In this case, it was a free-standing half-skeleton, half-human Neanderthal woman. He gasped and spun away, almost crashing into a stegosaurus, which had been reconstructed from thousands of tiny bones.

Link was surrounded by prehistoric images, which swirled around in front of his eyes like a nightmare. A sabertooth cat's skull. A rebuilt woolly mammoth. There were skulls and spears and fossils, memories surrounding him. Link stumbled away, growling from somewhere deep inside, a growl that was more like a primal scream.

Up around the corner, Jerry was pointing out artifacts to the class when Dave and Stoney heard the scream.

"Oh, no," Dave said, and grabbed Stoney, pulling him in the direction of the screaming.

Matt slipped away from the group, too, and followed them discreetly.

* * *

In the meantime, Link fell over a stuffed giant sloth, and he shrieked, knocking it the rest of the way to the floor. Then, he ran as fast as he could back towards the first diorama he had seen, the one that reminded him of home.

Dave and Stoney raced through the museum, looking for Link.

"He's gotta be around here *somewhere*," Dave said, out of breath.

Stoney nodded, and they kept running.

Matt, ducking behind columns to stay out of sight, followed them every step of the way.

Link burst into the diorama. Once he was inside, he jumped up and down, reverting to his original state. He tried to take a bite out of what looked like a piece of meat, but it was plastic. This angered him, and he threw it out of the diorama. He started ripping his clothes off, opting for an animal skin from one of the mannequins. He squatted over a pit and began to rub two sticks together, making a small fire.

He had gone back to the Ice Age.

* * *

Dave and Stoney were still frantically searching the corridors and exhibits. They didn't notice Matt hiding, but they *did* find Link, crying and hunched over his fire.

"There he is," Dave said.

Stoney nodded.

They stood a few feet away, not sure how to handle this.

"He knows, Dave," Stoney said. "He totally knows what happened to him. Come on, we've got to help him."

He crawled into the diorama, and Dave followed, helping him stamp out the fire. Then, they sat down next to Link who was very upset.

"It's okay, Link," Stoney said. "Here, look." He pointed to the mannequin family of Neanderthals. "Family." He pointed to Link, and then to himself. "Family." He pointed to Dave, and then to himself, and then to Link. "Family. Fam-i-ly. We are your new family." He pointed to the mannequin Neanderthals, and then made a circle around the three of them. *"Family."*

Link understood, pointing to the fake

Neanderthals and then to Dave and
Stoney. "Family," he said.

Dave nodded. "Yes."

"Family," Link said. He looked at the
fake Neanderthals, and then took Dave and
Stoney in his arms and hugged them
tightly. "Family. Family."

"Right," Stoney said, and they all burst
out laughing.

Matt watched this entire scene with his
mouth hanging open. Then, he turned and
ran off, careful not to let any of them see
him.

The posse was never going to believe *this*
one.

Chapter 15

After Link fell asleep that night in his cow pajamas, Dave and Stoney sat on the edge of Dave's bed, looking at the pictures they had taken of him so far.

Stoney shook his head, very concerned. "He's burnt from all this, man," he said. "Be a little more mellow on him."

Dave shrugged, still torn over the situation. "Considering we started this school year as losers, and now everyone knows who we are, I don't think one mistake is such a big deal."

"Dave, you're *dogging* him," Stoney said.

"Just promise me to be mellow with him. Not so much."

Dave sighed. "Stoney . . ."

"*Dave* . . ." Stoney said, with no humor in his voice.

Dave nodded reluctantly. "Okay. If it's going to make you feel better, I'll be mellow."

Stoney also nodded. Firmly.

They looked at Link, whose snores were very peaceful — and very loud.

Link's last class period at school the next day was driver's ed, which met out in the school parking lot. Mr. Beady, who was in his late fifties, was the teacher.

He stood in front of a battered student driver car, checking names off his attendance list.

"Okay, Robyn Sweeny?" he said.

Robyn emerged from the crowd of kids.

Mr. Beady frowned at her. "*Again?*"

"Sorry," she said, flushing slightly. "I just can't get that parallel parking thing going."

He frowned, but then checked her off,

118

and she got into the car. Mr. Beady looked back down at his list.

"Linkavitch Chomofsky!" he read.

Link smiled and stepped forward.

Dave and Stoney were inside the school in their English class.

Stoney, who was sitting by the window, happened to glance out. Seeing Link with Mr. Beady and the others, he leaned forward to nudge Dave.

"Buddy, you promised me mellow," he whispered. "That isn't *mellow*."

Dave looked outside, then shrugged. "No problem," he said.

"Okay," Mr. Beady was saying, down in the parking lot. "Get in the car."

Link smiled devilishly, and climbed into the driver's seat.

Just then, sitting safely in their English class, Dave and Stoney looked at each other in horror, as a thought occurred to them.

The only time Link had ever been behind the wheel was when he played — Rad Mobile!

"Oh, no," Dave said, with a sinking feeling in his stomach.

"Rad Mobile!" Stoney yelled, and their teacher and the rest of the class stared as they tore out of the classroom.

They raced outside, making a beeline for the parking lot, and managed to jump into the backseat of the car just as Link put it in gear. Then, as Mr. Beady screamed "No!", Link hit the accelerator, and the car peeled out of the parking lot with Dave still halfway out the door.

Stoney, now in the front seat, tried to get control of the dual steering wheel as Link careened around the school grounds, laughing his head off.

"Tell him to stop!" Dave yelled.

"Okay." Stoney turned to Link. "Stop!"

Link kept driving, and Stoney looked at Dave.

"Didn't faze him, bro," he said.

Dave was still struggling to get all the way inside the car and slam the door. "Take the wheel!" he shouted. "Do *something*!"

Stoney grabbed the wheel, and the car lurched up on one side. Everyone outside scattered as the driver's ed car drove on two wheels down the middle of the walkway. Teachers shrieked and ducked, while students cheered Link on.

"What is he doing?!" Robyn asked, hanging on to the backseat for dear life.

Dave, who had finally managed to get all of the way in, looked over. "Driving," he said. "Badly!"

"This is the way they drive in his country, Robyn!" Stoney yelled from the front.

One of the science teachers moved out to stop them, waving his clipboard frantically.

"Stop that car, young man!" he ordered.

Link stuck his head out the car window, leaning one elbow on the door. "Outta da way!" he said with a perfect Brooklyn accent.

Then, he pulled his head back in and laughed, enjoying this new three-dimensional version of Rad Mobile. He *liked* this game!

They swerved down Encino Boulevard, past befuddled motorists and pedestrians, the car still up on two wheels.

The traffic light ahead of them turned

yellow, and then red, and Robyn screamed.

"Red light!" She covered her eyes. "Ahhh!"

Link slammed on the brakes, and the car stopped inches from the crosswalk — still teetering up on two wheels. Now, they all screamed in unison. Dave poked his head out to survey the situation.

"Don't anybody breathe!" he warned.

The car swayed back and forth, and they all stayed perfectly still and silent, listening to the car creak.

"Okay," Dave whispered. "Breathe left. No, breathe right, no, Link, breathe *my* right!"

They all expelled their breath to the right, and that was all it took to make the car lose its balance. Dave ducked his head inside as the car rolled over — a full one hundred and eighty degrees — landing on its *other* two wheels.

The traffic light turned green, and Link drove off as though nothing had happened, leaving another car that was idling next to them in the dust.

As it happened, that car was being driven by Mrs. Morgan, who watched the driver's ed car skate away on two wheels. Then, she looked over at Teena, who was sitting in the passenger's seat, listening to her Walkman.

"I think when it's your time to drive, we'll get you a private instructor," she said.

Teena nodded vaguely, half asleep behind a pair of sunglasses.

Back at the school, there were now several police cars parked in the lot. Mr. Beady and a few kids pointed in the direction of the lost driver's ed car, and gave statements to various bored officers.

As a Rad Mobile champion, Link was always looking for new challenges, and so he drove, and drove, and drove. By now, they were somewhere deep in the San Fernando Valley, which was completely unfamiliar territory for all of them. It was getting dark, a storm was brewing, and they were in a *very* questionable neighborhood.

The car was flying along down the street when Robyn suddenly reached over and turned the key. The car slammed its way right into a parking space — and died.

Link stayed behind the wheel, still steering, not seeming to understand that the car wasn't moving anymore.

Nobody spoke for a long minute.

"That concludes our parallel parking lesson for today," Stoney said, breaking the silence. Then, he paused. "Class dismissed."

Dave and Robyn smiled weakly.

Chapter 16

They all sat there for another minute.

Then Robyn laughed. "Hey, Link, I think you just failed driver's ed."

"Well." Dave unclenched his fists from their death grip around the door handle. "At least we didn't total the car."

They got out, and saw that the car had been completely — totaled.

Robyn laughed again, and Link picked her up, spinning her around in a happy dance. For him, it had been a wonderful afternoon.

Stoney dragged Dave off to one side.

"I *told* you he was edged," he said. "You

never listen to me. I'm a unique weasel with far too much insight, and you never listen to me."

Dave thought that over. "When don't I listen to you? When have I *ever* not listened to you?" He turned to find Link, to get outside confirmation of this fact. "Link, don't I always — " He stopped.

Link was gone.

Robyn pointed down the street.

"He went in there," she said.

A few feet down the block, loud music spilled out of a rowdy-looking bar. A few drunken patrons stumbled out of it and into the street.

Stoney sighed. "Come on, bro. Let's go get him."

As Stoney went into the bar, Dave stayed out on the street with Robyn.

"Why can't things go smoothly for once?" he asked. "Just *once*?"

Robyn smiled at him. "Dave, it's going to be okay."

Dave just sat down on the sidewalk and put his head in his hands.

"For *you*, it's going to be okay," he said.

"I'm just your typical high school droid without any real future."

Robyn sat next to him, not sure what to say. She almost didn't know how to respond to him when he was acting . . . human.

"Dave," she said finally. "This isn't the real world. You can only be captain of the football team for so long. You're probably better off than the rest of us." She paused. "Don't worry so much, Dave."

"Yeah, maybe." He looked over. "When this is all over, maybe I could sit at your lunch table?"

She looked back at him very seriously, *really* seeing him for the first time in ages, then pushed a strand of hair off his face. He was about to say something, when the sound of screaming came from the bar. The moment was broken and Robyn stood up, brushing herself off.

"Come on," she said, and held her hand out. "We'd better get those guys."

Dave took her hand, and they walked into the bar.

The bar was bright and colorful, and filled with men and women drinking and dancing. The whole place had a Caribbean flavor. Loud music was blasting from the speakers. Vats of *salsa* and *chile con queso* lined the bar, and *margaritas* were being poured liberally.

Link and Stoney were at the bar, surrounded by three men — Enrique, Loco, and Chuy. A new song started playing and, seeing people headed for the dance floor, Link went out to join them.

Left alone with the three strangers, Stoney shifted in his seat uncomfortably.

"*Órale vatos*, dudes," he said, putting on a smile.

Meanwhile, Matt and his posse had broken into the Encino High attendance office as soon as it got dark. They stood in front of a file cabinet. Phil held a flashlight as Matt went through the files.

"Chomofsky . . ." he said aloud, searching. "Chomofsky . . ." He thumbed through the records until he found the file that read *Chomofsky, Linkavitch.* "Got it!"

"Good," Phil said.

"Way to go," Will said.

"Yup," Bill said.

Matt opened the file and started reading it.

"What the . . . rabies?" He stopped, baffled. "Distemper? A *flea dip*? What is this?" He peeled off a Publisher's Clearing House sticker to reveal the Encino Department of Animal Regulation logo.

Will leaned over to look. "It's a dog license, man."

"Whoa," Phil said, not knowing what the implications of that were — but knowing that there must *be* some.

"Maybe he's a dog," Bill said after a pause, and Will and Phil nodded.

"L.A. County Animal Shelter," Matt read from the bottom of the form. "Okay, so what are the two biggest losers in school hiding?"

They all frowned.

Quickly, Matt pocketed the papers, and he and the posse left the office, undetected.

Dave and Robyn walked into the bar, hand in hand, looking for Stoney and Link.

They located Stoney at the bar, and walked over.

Stoney lifted an eyebrow at them. "So, what have *you* guys been doing?" he asked slyly.

Dave ignored that, and scanned the room. "Where's Link?"

Stoney gestured towards the dance floor, where Link was grooving to the music.

Robyn pulled on Dave's arm.

"Come on," she said. "Let's dance."

Dave shook his head. "I don't dance. I *hate* dancing."

Robyn looked at him in exasperation. "Dave, you're *so* uptight," she said.

With that parting shot, she went out to the dance floor to join Link, and Dave sat down at the bar to sulk.

Enrique, who had a row of shots of *tequila* lined up in front of him, looked over at Stoney. "You want to be a man?"

"Uh, ultimately, yeah," Stoney said.

"Then, drink like a man," Chuy said, and took a shot.

"*Hombre, un macho,*" Loco said, and downed another one of the glasses.

Stoney shook his head and put the glass down.

Dave missed all of this because he was watching as Link and Robyn mixed it up on the dance floor. Link was leading the whole crowd, and they were all having a blast.

"Go for it!" someone yelled, dancing.

"Shake it, mon!" another admirer chimed in.

Link started dancing his caveman dance and quickly the other people in the bar caught on and began doing it, too. Caught up in the fun, María, Enrique's girlfriend, joined Link and Robyn, and they all danced together, having the time of their lives.

When the song ended, Robyn and Link ran off the dance floor, over to Dave and Stoney.

Dave turned to yell at Robyn for abandoning him.

"Link and I were just dancing, Dave," she said before he could start. "Relax."

"Link. Link." Dave aimed a kick at the nearest bar stool. "I'm sick of hearing about *Link* all the time. Stop trying to compare me to him. Link isn't what you think he is."

Robyn shrugged, not caring one way or the other what Link was. "Whatever," she said. "But at least Link is a free spirit. He's not concerned with what everyone else thinks. At least *he* knows how to have fun." She tossed her hair back, and walked out of the bar.

Dave just stood there.

"I can have fun," he said quietly and uncertainly.

Just then, someone screamed near the front door.

"Police," the bartender yelled, so all of the patrons would hear him.

The bar erupted into mass confusion, as everyone tried to get out at once, knocking chairs, tables, and other people out of the way in their haste.

"Oh, no," Dave said, and looked around for Link.

Link was swinging from a light fixture, and Dave ran over to try and pull him down.

"Link, get down!" he bellowed. "Get down! We're going to get busted."

"You *are* busted," an angry voice behind him said.

Dave turned around and saw a cop standing there.

He was busted.

Chapter 17

Dave and Link were arrested and taken to the police station to be booked. Once they were inside, Dave's fingerprints were taken first, and then it was Link's turn. But Link was fascinated by the well of ink, and he used it to finger paint. An officer took his fingers out of the ink, and Link smiled, and ran his hands down Dave's face, smudging him.

"I know my rights!" Dave shouted as he was dragged down the hall to have his mug shot taken. "No one's Mirandized me! I get a phone call, you know!"

None of the police officers paid the slightest bit of attention to this.

Officer Sims, the man who had just taken Link's fingerprints, studied the card with a puzzled frown.

"How strange . . ." he said quietly, and looked at the card more closely.

They were not like any fingerprints he had ever seen.

Down in the mug shot room, Dave held up a card with numbers, waiting, with his shoulders slumped, to have his picture taken. Just as the camera was about to go off, Link stuck his body into the frame, put his arm around Dave's shoulder, and gave the camera a great big smile.

The camera flashed, and the moment was preserved permanently.

Robyn ended up driving Enrique's car to her house, with Enrique and Stoney, who had both escaped the melee at the bar. She tried to park, but steered the car onto the sidewalk — parallel parking really was a big problem for her. But she just got out of the car, waved gaily, and Enrique and

Stoney drove off together, the tires bumping over the curb.

She walked up her driveway and found Matt sitting on the front steps, waiting for her.

"Nice element you're hanging out with," Matt said. "Who was the guy in the low rider?"

Robyn fumbled for her keys and started to open the door. "None of your business."

Matt came after her. "What time do you want me to pick you up tomorrow night? It's the Prom, remember?"

Robyn turned to face him, completely fed up with everyone and everything.

"You know what, Matt?" she said. "You're just like everyone else. All you care about is what other people think. It's pathetic."

Matt scowled, his fists tightening automatically. "Hey, watch it . . ."

"And you know what else?" Robyn went on. "I'm not going to the Prom with you. I'm going with a guy who's really cool and not afraid of being himself, or having fun."

Then, she went inside and slammed the door in his face.

Matt stood there, stunned.

"Who's cooler than *me*?" he said after her.

"Link," Robyn said through the door.

Matt was even more stunned. "That guy?"

"Totally," Robyn said, and turned off the porch lights, leaving him in the dark.

"He's *bagged*," Matt said, and stormed away from the house.

At the police station, Dave and Link were handcuffed to a bench, sort of. Link's handcuffs hadn't been tightened, and they clicked open. He examined them, looked at Dave's, and then shut his again. This time, they locked.

Dave slumped on the bench, staring straight ahead at nothing.

"You're getting to be a real pain, you know that?" he said. "We wouldn't even *be* here if you didn't have to swing from a stupid chandelier, and steal the driver's ed car, and — "

Link looked over. "Dave?"

"What?" Dave asked sulkily.

"Shut up, Dave," Link said.

Dave's mouth dropped open. "What? Nice. Really nice thing to say to the guy who dug you out of the ground."

Link shrugged, and they both slumped miserably on the bench.

By the time Officer Sims came to get Dave for his phone call, Link had fallen asleep on his shoulder.

"Hey, man," Dave said, trying to get up. "This isn't due process. I'm gonna get released on a technicality, so you might as well just let me go, pal."

Officer Sims didn't acknowledge that. He unlocked their handcuffs and shook Link awake.

"Come with me," he said.

Dave and Link followed him around the corner to a pay phone, where Officer Sims stopped.

"Your phone call," he said. "You only have one. Make it quick."

Dave felt in his pockets for change, then looked up sheepishly. Officer Sims rolled his eyes, and handed him a quarter. Link just burped.

Dave used the quarter to call Robyn.

"Hi," he said when she answered. "It's Dave."

"Dave! Did you guys get away okay?" she asked.

Dave moved his jaw, still repressing the urge to *slug* Link. "Not," he said. "We're in prison. And let me tell you, it's been great. Really great."

"Oh, no," Robyn said.

Link was trying to take the phone from him, and Dave elbowed him away.

"Knock it off!" he said as Link kept trying.

"What?" Robyn asked, not sure what she had done.

"Nothing. Link wants the phone." Dave shoved him harder. "But he can't have it!"

Link burped, right in his face.

"That's really funny," Dave said, not even remotely amused.

"Dave, what are you talking about?" Robyn asked, trying to figure out what was going on.

Dave sighed. "Look, this is my one phone call. And I'm using it to ask you to go to the Prom with me, so just say yes."

Robyn hesitated. "No," she said.

Dave stared at the phone in his hand. *"What?"*

"I want to ask Link," she said. "Look, ask Link if he'll go with me."

Dave blinked at the receiver, genuinely stunned. *"You want me to what?"*

"I — " Robyn let out her breath. "I just want to have fun, I don't want to turn this into a big deal. Link's fun, and he won't take it seriously. *You'll* probably have a seizure or something."

Dave shook his head, trying to clear it, hoping that she was kidding. "I — that's not funny, Robyn."

"Lighten up, Dave," she said. "Who cares about the stupid Prom, anyway. Look, we'll all go together, how's that?"

"Unacceptable," he said stiffly.

There was an ugly silence.

"Well," she said. "I don't know what to say."

"Say nothing. I'm hanging up now." Dave hung up the phone and glared at Link, trying to figure out how he could have betrayed him like that. "You *dissed* me, man," he said quietly.

Link smiled at him, and burped, completely uncomprehending.

An hour later, Dave's parents showed up to bail them out. Mr. Morgan bundled his coat around Link's shoulders as they left the station. Thunder rumbled somewhere off in the distance as lightning flashed across the night sky.

"Are you two all right?" Mrs. Morgan asked anxiously.

Dave shrugged, too angry and upset by the whole evening to look at them. "Sure, Mom, we're great," he said. "Jail's been a lot of fun."

Mr. Morgan scowled at him. "Don't talk to your mother like that." He put his arm protectively around Link. "This boy is a guest in our home. We are accountable for him, and you go off and pull a stunt like this!"

"I didn't — " Dave protested. "I — "

"I don't understand, David," his mother said, her expression very disappointed. "You *stole* a car?"

The whole thing was too complicated to

explain, so Dave just shook his head. "It was an accident."

"Stealing a car is an accident?" his father said, his voice rising with every syllable. "Destroying school property is an accident? Getting a phone call in the middle of the night is an *accident*?"

Dave sighed, suddenly feeling *extremely* tired. "Dad . . ."

"All right, Larry," Mrs. Morgan said. "Let's just go home and sort this out."

"He's going to pay for this out of his own allowance," Mr. Morgan muttered.

"Let's just go," Mrs. Morgan said and led Dave to the car.

When they got to the house, Dave's parents spent the next hour or so trying to "sort things out," but mostly just yelling at him. Finally, he was sent to bed, and wasn't surprised to find Link already fast asleep, wrapped in a small afghan.

Dave watched him for a minute. He folded his arms angrily across his chest.

"Yeah," he whispered. "All three of us should go to the Prom together. Sure. . . . You're messing everything up, man. And I can't take you to Letterman 'cause then you'll get famous and she'll like you even more."

Link slept on, blasting a loud snore every so often.

"I don't know what to do with you," Dave whispered. "I just can't take care of you anymore."

Outside, it began to rain much harder, and water started trickling into Dave's pool.

Chapter 18

As soon as it was light out, Dave took Link out to the car and put him inside, fastening the seat belt over him. Stoney rode up the street on his scooter just as Dave was getting into the car. He yelled, trying to get Dave's attention. Dave glanced at him for a second, but then just got into the car, slammed his door, and drove away.

Stoney sat on his scooter by the curb, trying to figure out what was going on.

Dave drove for a long time, then took an exit off the interstate highway onto a barren road.

"It's just that things didn't turn out

right," he said aloud. "And I don't want them cutting you into little pieces or anything, so this is the best thing for all of us."

Link sat up front very quietly, with a knapsack and a skateboard in his lap.

"Best for you, best for me," Dave said. "I just don't know how else to help you anymore."

Link sat there, wide-eyed and silent.

"I really don't know what else to do," Dave said. He pulled off the road, stopped the car, and leaned over to open Link's door. "Okay, Link. Out."

Link just sat there.

Dave gently pushed him out, and Link stood at the side of the road with a small, lost expression on his face.

"Here." Dave handed him a bunch of quarters. "For Rad Mobile."

He gave him a little shove, and Link took the quarters and began walking very slowly down the long, dusty road.

Suddenly, Stoney drove up on his scooter, looking like Rommel of the Desert with raccoon eyes. When he saw Link walking away, he knew what was going down, and he jumped off his scooter. He ran over to the car and stood face to face with Dave, trying to control himself.

"What are you doing?" he demanded.

Dave wouldn't look at him. "I'm letting him go," he said. "I can't handle him anymore, Stone. He'll be better off with someone else."

Stoney stared at him, then shook his head vehemently. "Okay, buddy. I've let you take this far enough. Call him back."

Dave shook his head even more vehemently. "No. I can't do it anymore."

"I'm not kidding, Dave," Stoney said. "Call him back."

Dave started to get back into his car. "It's done, man."

Stoney grabbed him by the arm and spun him around, slamming him up against the hood as hard as he could.

"You know that's harsh," Stoney said through his teeth. "You weez off of Link's gig because you think he can *get you somewhere*. And then, when he gets crusty, you bag him." He twisted his hand in Dave's shirt to keep him from moving away. "That's *not* happening, Dave. That's not how it works with friends. Friends don't dog each other. You stand by your friends, no matter what — you don't bag them because they get in your way!"

"Get off me, man!" Dave gave him an angry shove in return. "What do you care? You've never cared about anything in your life except nugs, chillin', and grindage."

"Well, I care now!" Stoney said.

Dave knocked his hand off his shirt. "You're just as selfish as I am, man. You just *hide* it better."

Stoney shook his head, his eyes very sad as he looked at his old friend. "That's fully untrue."

"You came along for the ride," Dave said pugnaciously, "and you let *me* do all the dirty work 'cause maybe it'd work out to your advantage."

Stoney looked at him with utter disgust. "Those are the desperate words of a loser," he said, spitting out the words. "Maybe Matt Wilson was right about you all along."

Dave grabbed him by the shirt collar, and Stoney swung at him. Then they started fighting, yelling at each other and exchanging hard punches.

Down the road, Link stopped walking

when he heard the sounds of the fight.

"Take that back!" Dave shouted.

"No." Stoney punched him. "You."

"No." Dave punched him twice as hard. "You!"

Link ran back to the car and tried to pull them apart. "Family!"

Dave and Stoney didn't even hear him as they rolled and struggled in the dirt.

"Fam-i-ly!" Link yelled, and yanked Dave away from Stoney, holding on to him tightly. "Family. Family."

"Let go of me!" Dave said, out of breath. "Stop it!"

Stoney stood up, a little wobbly, wiping blood from his nose. Dave was still fighting to get away, but Link hung on.

"Family — Dave," he said fiercely into Dave's ear. "Family — Stoney."

"I don't care what you say! I — " Dave stopped suddenly, realizing what he had just done. He looked at Stoney, whose nose had bled onto his shirt, and then he looked at Link, who was close to tears. "Stoney, I — I — " He couldn't think of anything to say, knowing that all of this was his fault.

Stoney just shivered a little, and pressed his sleeve against his nose.

"Okay." Dave let out his breath. His whole body sagged. "I'm okay. Link, you can let go."

Link released him, his expression flooded with remorse.

"I'm sorry, man," Dave said to him. "I'm really sorry."

Link hugged him with one arm, then grabbed Stoney and hugged him with his other arm. Then they all separated, and Dave and Stoney looked at each other. They had been friends for a very long time. . . .

Slowly, they both smiled.

"Who needs the Prom, man?" Dave said. "Let's go home."

Stoney and Link nodded, and they one-hand snapped. Then, Link opened the driver's door to get into the car.

"Uh, thanks, Link," Dave said. "But this time, I think *I'll* drive."

Chapter 19

That evening, Dave helped Link get ready for the Prom. He was wearing a psychedelic sixties-type tux, with Day-Glo orange sneakers, and his hair hung wild and free around his shoulders. He looked, in a word, *fabu*.

"You look good," Dave said.

Link reached over and tapped Dave's T-shirt.

Dave shook his head. "Can't go, man."

"Go, man," Link said pleadingly.

"Can't. You go. Have a great time for me." Dave smiled at him. "You deserve it."

Downstairs, the doorbell rang, and Teena answered it. Robyn was standing there, looking terrific.

"Hi," she said.

Teena nodded, surveying her gown with a rather critical eye. "Hey."

Link came downstairs, and sniffed Robyn's hair.

"Hi, Link," Robyn said.

Dave came down behind him, with the camera.

"Here." He handed it to Robyn. "Take lots of pictures of Link. For the yearbook." He grinned wryly. "He'll probably get his own page."

"Come with us," Robyn said. "We'll have fun."

"Sorry. Can't." Dave shrugged, indicating the living room, where his parents were. "Grounded. Probation. Jailed. Never allowed to leave the house again. But . . . have fun." He smiled at them, and gave Link a gentle push out the door and down the front walk.

After Link had left with Robyn, Stoney came over, and he and Dave reclined in lawn chairs in the backyard, looking up at the sky. The pool was still only half dug, and filled with muddy water from the previous night's rain. A few paper lanterns blew in the breeze.

And — except for the two of them — there was no one else there to enjoy it.

"Some stupid party, hunh?" Dave said.

Stoney nodded. "Yeah."

"I was supposed to have Robyn, we were supposed to go to the Prom together, and this was *supposed* to be the party to end all parties," Dave said.

"Yeah." Stoney tossed a pebble into the pool, and it landed with a dull plop. "We ended up with a caveman, instead."

Dave nodded, and tossed a pebble of his own. "I don't regret it, do you?"

"Nope," Stoney said. "I don't regret it."

They raised their glasses to toast.

"To Link," Dave said. "May he have a cool time at the Prom."

"To Linkage!" Stoney agreed.

They drank their sodas.

"Hey," Dave said. "There's always college."

Stoney grinned sheepishly. "Or . . . junior college."

They one-hand snapped.

When Link and Robyn walked into the Prom, they were quickly surrounded by kids from every clique. All of them were happy to see Link, and they parted like the Red Sea to let him through. Only Ella stood on the sidelines, frowning.

Link was easily the most popular caveman in school.

Matt and Phil, both wearing tacky tuxedos, drove to Dave's house, looking for Link.

"Hey!" Matt called softly, standing below Dave's bedroom window. "Link! You loser! Get out here!"

"He's hiding in his room," Phil said. "Go get him!"

Matt was taken aback by that. "Get him?"

"Yeah, man," Phil said. "The guy's not coming down. He's going to the Prom with your lady, is he not?"

"Yeah . . ." Matt said, and looked up at the dark window without enthusiasm.

"And after the Prom, you *know* he's going to take the lady out," Phil said.

Matt doubled up his fist. "Watch it."

Phil was unimpressed. "Hey — I'm not the one you want, man."

Matt nodded uncertainly. "Okay. Yeah," he said. "I'm goin'."

When he didn't move, Phil folded his arms.

"I'm going, I'm going," Matt said, and began to crawl up the nearest tree.

Once he was close enough to the window, Matt jimmied it open and slid into Dave's room. It was dark but, in the reflection of the moonlight, Matt could see the prehistoric hovel that had once been a plain bedroom.

"Slob," he said.

He almost stepped on the Mousterian bowl, and he kicked it aside. He crept around until he stumbled upon a toolbox that said *Private Property* across the top.

"*Hel*-lo," Matt said, and tried to open it.

The box was locked, but he banged it on the floor until the lock broke. Inside, there were pictures of: Link, encased in ice; Link being pulled out of the pool; and Link in the toolshed, defrosting. Each picture was dated, and had notes written on the back about the discovery of Link. Matt flicked on a flashlight to study them more closely.

"Whoa," he said, and shoved the photos into his pocket.

He couldn't wait to go blow the guy's cover.

Lying out in the backyard, Dave noticed a light in his bedroom window, then he heard Boris barking. He leaped out of his chair and dashed into the house.

"Stone! Trouble!" he shouted back over his shoulder, as he ran upstairs.

But, outside, they could hear Matt's Corvette starting up.

"Come on!" Stoney said, and they ran outdoors.

Dave got to the car just as Matt was about to take off. Matt laughed, and waved the pictures at him.

"Give them back!" Dave grabbed onto the car door. "They're mine!"

"See ya, loser," Matt said, gunned his engine and sped away.

In the driveway, Stoney already had the car started, and Dave jumped in. Stoney stomped on the accelerator and they followed the Corvette, careening through the night.

At the school gym, the Prom was in full swing. Robyn and Link were up on a makeshift stage, and Robyn had a crown on her head. They were both sitting on small thrones. Despite just having been selected as the Prom Queen, Robyn looked tired and a little bit sad.

Kim, the senior class president, was also on the stage, making the Prom King announcement over a handheld mike.

"And it's unanimous," he said. "The vote for Prom King goes to — "

A girl was about to put the crown on Link's head when the back doors of the gym swung open, revealing Matt and Phil.

"Wait! Wait!" Matt pushed his way through the crowd and jumped up onto the stage, clutching the pictures in his hand. He grabbed Link by the collar and held him up in front of the crowd. "This is our school, right, everyone?"

Link didn't like being grabbed, and he growled, trying to twist free.

"And we should know," Matt went on, "if something bogus is going down in our school, right?"

There was no response. Everyone looked confused.

"Right!" Phil, Bill, and Will bellowed.

"Well, let me tell you something." Matt held up the pictures in his free hand. "There has been something bogus going on in our school. Something heinous. We've all been taken for a ride. Taken for *suckers*."

The crowd mumbled and grumbled, wondering what he was talking about.

"This hummer's taken you for a ride!" Matt proclaimed, pointing at Link with his free hand. "His name isn't Linkavitch Chomofsky! And he's not from Estonia! He's been *lying* to us."

"What are you talking about?" Ella asked.

"They've all been lying to us," Matt said. "They think we're idiots, but we're not. *I* found out. *I* know the truth!"

Robyn sat on her throne, staring at him, frozen.

"Do you want the truth?" Matt asked. "Do you want to know what he really is?"

"Yeah!" the crowd said in unison.

"He's a *caveman!*" Matt shouted at the top of his lungs.

There was a pause, and then an explosion of noise.

"*COOL!!!*" everyone yelled.

Chapter 20

The music came back on, and everyone started dancing again as though nothing at all strange had happened.

Matt stood on the stage, perplexed.

"No! I'm serious!" he said, trying to get their attention again. "Look — I've got pictures!"

Just as he said that, Dave jumped onto the stage and blindsided him so that the pictures flew out of his hands. In the ensuing confusion, Robyn bent down and picked them up.

Matt turned to see Dave. "Out of my

way," he said, then punched Dave square in the face.

Dave was knocked off the makeshift stage. Kids crowded around to help him up.

During all of this, Robyn looked at the pictures, looked at Link, and looked back at the pictures.

"Oh, wow," she said, and tucked the pictures into her dress, out of sight.

Link went after Matt. He lifted Matt up and spun him around his head like Dave had taught him during their wrestling session. Matt tried to gain control, but Link was too strong for him. Phil, Bill, and Will did their best to help Matt, but the crowd formed a human wall and held them back as Link tossed Matt into the large cake on the refreshments table.

The crowd cheered, and Stoney picked up a ladle of punch from the punchbowl and poured it on Matt's face for good measure. Everyone applauded, and Stoney winked at Link, then took a bow.

Kim, resuming his duties as class president, picked up the microphone.

"Well, that was the unscheduled entertainment portion of our evening," he said. "And now, we're supposed to have our Prom King and Queen lead a slow one." He paused for effect. "May I present Robyn Sweeny and Linkavitch Chomofsky, Encino High's royalty!"

A spotlight came on, and everyone clapped as Robyn and Link began to dance. But Link glanced over at Dave, who was standing next to Stoney and looking very solemn. So, Link danced Robyn over to him and twirled her into his arms.

"Family," Link said to them, and smiled. He took off his crown and put it on Dave's head instead. "Fresh nugs," Link whispered. "Mmmm."

Everyone clapped, and Dave and Robyn began to dance together.

They slow-danced under the soft spotlight, with a definite spark between them, as the senior class looked on, smiling. Link and Stoney one-hand snapped. Then, Link moved onto the dance floor to cut in on Robyn and Dave. It looked as though he was going to dance with her, but instead he took Dave away from Robyn and slow-danced with *him*.

Everyone cracked up.

After the Prom, everyone went back to Dave's house for a party. There was a caravan of cars and limos, with Link leading the pack in the AMC Matador. They all danced and laughed and chased each other, jumping in and out of the muddy pool. Jerry was there, and Enrique and María, and everyone else Link had met so far in Encino. Even Rajnish and Kashmir had shown up to join the fun.

To Stoney's delight, Amy, the waitress from Blades, had come, and from the moment she arrived he danced with her nonstop.

Everyone at the party was having fun. They might even have been having *too* much fun, as they splashed in the muddy pool, threw Frisbees, and overate. The yard was never going to be the same.

Ella came over to interrupt Robyn and Dave, who were dancing by the swing set.

"Excuse us," she said to Dave, and pulled Robyn over behind the slide. "*This* is what you left Matt for? In your peak year, for *David Morgan*?"

Robyn nodded. "Yeah. Because this isn't my peak year, Ella. I've got my whole life to peak. And I'm going to do it with people who care about me. Right now, I'm just not sure you're one of them." Then, she turned around and went back to Dave.

Ella stood by the slide, totally shocked.

Taking advantage of this, Teena walked up behind her and pushed her into the pool. She was *much* more amused than Ella was.

As the party went on, Jerry Brushe, acting as a chaperon, wandered around in search of something good to eat. He found some chips and, as his hands touched the bowl, he bent to look at it more closely. His eyes widened as he held the bowl up to the moonlight, peering at it from every angle.

It was — a Mousterian bowl!

It was getting late, and Dave and Robyn walked together in the front yard, hand in hand.

"You totally protected him, didn't you," she said.

Dave flushed a little, remembering their

morning trip to the highway. "Not totally."

"What you did was very cool," Robyn said.

"Really?" Realizing he sounded too eager, Dave shrugged instead. "Hey, who cares about cool, anyway." He paused. "Of course, there *is* one really cool thing I'd like to show you."

"What?" Robyn asked, looking around.

"This," Dave said, and took her in his arms and kissed her.

When they broke apart, Robyn was smiling.

"Cool," she said.

They kissed again.

Out in the backyard, where the festivities were still in full swing, everyone was now doing the caveman dance, following Link's lead.

It was the party to end all parties.

By dawn, the party had finally wound down and Dave, Robyn, Stoney, and Link were the only ones left in the yard. They were all asleep on lawn chairs.

Then, a rumbling tremor rocked the

earth and the muddy water in the pool started draining out.

The vibrations jolted Link and Stoney awake.

When the tremor subsided, Dave and Robyn, who hadn't even felt it, sleepily woke up. Dave yawned widely, then pointed at the pool. "Hey, look!" he said.

Chunks of ice had floated to the surface of the pool and were glistening in the morning light. Then, a very *large* block popped up, sparkling brightly.

"Whoa," Dave said, along with everyone else.

There seemed to be something inside the block of ice, and they all moved to the edge of the pool to take a closer look.

When Link saw what was inside, he threw his head back and howled with glee. He jumped up and down, trying to pull the block of ice out of the water. When Dave, Stoney, and Robyn realized what he was looking at, they all smiled.

Embedded in the block of ice was . . . *a cavewoman!*